GOD DESIRES YOU

Eunan Mc Donnell SDB

God Desires You

ST FRANCIS DE SALES ON LIVING THE GOSPEL

the columba press

First published in 2001 by
the columba press
55A Spruce Avenue, Stillorgan Industrial Park,
Blackrock, Co Dublin

Cover by Bill Bolger
Origination by The Columba Press
Printed in Ireland by Colour Books Ltd, Dublin

ISBN 1 85607 343 2

Acknowledgements

I would like to thank all those who assisted me in helping this
book become a reality. In particular the Visitation Sisters of
Stamullen, who were the original inspiration for writing this
book. It was in delivering a series of conferences on St Francis
de Sales to them, that the genesis of this book appeared. Also the
Visitation Sisters of Partridge Green have been a help and
inspiration. A special word of thanks to A. Pocetto who not only
encouraged me, but was extremely helpful in leading me to various resources. Finally, I would like to thank various individuals
for their encouragement and support: Sr Catherine OCD, Sr Mary
Bridget FMA, Ellie O' Dwyer and Rev Denis Robinson SDB.

Contents

*Dedicated to the
Sisters of the Visitation,
Stamullen, Co Meath,
Ireland*

The primary source for our study is the Annecy edition of the complete works of St Francis de Sales:

Oeuvres de Saint François de Sales, Edition Complète d'après les autographes et les èditions originales, Par les soins religeuses de la Visitation, du Premier Monastère d'Annecy, 1892-1964. 27 volumes.

A total of twenty-six volumes, with the recent addition of a most helpful index (vol 27) the *Oeuvres* include all existing manuscripts coming directly and indirectly from the pen of St Francis de Sales and generally accepted as the most authentic collection of Salesian writings.

The volumes of the Annecy Edition are as follows:

> I *Les Controverses*
> II *Defense de L'Estendart de la Sainte Croix*
> III *Introduction à la Vie Dévote*
> IV-V *Traitté de l'Amour de Dieu*
> VI *Les Vrays Entretiens Spirituels*
> VII-X *Sermons*
> XI-XXI *Lettres*
> XXII-XXVI *Opuscules*
> XXVII *Table Analytique*

As clearly indicated above, the *Treatise* is to be found in volumes IV and V of the Annecy edition. Our references shall be to the Annecy Edition, but the translations will be taken from *The Treatise on the Love of God*, J. K. Ryan trans., Rockford, Illinois: Tan Book and Publishers, Inc., 1975. Volumes I and II.

We will also be using J. K. Ryan's translation of *The*

Introduction To the Devout Life, New York, Image Books, 1972, which is vol III of the Annecy editions.

Eunan Mc Donnell SDB

ST FRANCIS DE SALES (1567-1622)

1567: 21 August, born at Thorens, the eldest of thirteen children. Thorens is in Savoy, present day eastern France and western Switzerland.

1577: First communion and confirmation.

1578: 25 September, leaves for College of Clermont at Paris, where he begins his course in humanities.

1584: Beginning of philosophical and theological studies at Paris, attends Genebrard's lectures on The Song of Songs.

1586-1587: December-January, temptation at Paris, spiritual crisis.

1588: 26 December, leaves for Padua where he studies law and theology.

1590-1591: His spiritual crisis returns at Padua.

1593: Ordained to the priesthood in the diocese of Geneva.

1594: Begins a four year mission in the Chablais region of Savoy to restore those who had fallen away from Catholicism to Calvinism. There are several attempts on his life during this period.

1595: Begins to edit the *Controverses* leaflets he had disseminated to explain the teachings of the Catholic Church.

1597: Engages in dialogue with Beza, the Calvinist leader of Geneva. Begins writing *Defence of the Cross*.

1602: Preaches Lenten sermons at Paris and frequents the salon of Mme Acarie.

1602: 8 December, consecrated Bishop of Geneva at Thorens.

1604: First sketches of *The Introduction to the Devout Life*, a collection of letters he had sent to various directees which he edits. They are directed to all people in every state of life, convinced that holiness is for all.

1604: Meets Jane Frances Freymot, Baroness de Chantal at Dijon, agrees to become her spiritual director.

1608: First publication of *The Introduction to the Devout Life*.

1609: Carries out the reform of the Abbey of Talloires.

1610: Foundation of the Sisters of the Visitation.

1614: Begins work on *The Treatise on the Love of God*.

1615: Calumniated before the Duke of Savoy.

1616: First publication of *The Treatise on the Love of God*.

1622: Refuses archbishopric of Turin.

1622: 28 December, dies of cerebal hemorrhage in Lyons, France.

1665: 19 April, canonised. His feast day is celebrated on 24 January.

1877: Proclaimed Doctor of the Church.

1923: Made Patron of Catholic journalists.

1967: Apostolic letter of Pope Paul VI.

1986: Pope John Paul II visits Lyons and Annecy and extols Francis as 'a precursor of Vatican II' and 'model for bishops because he was so completely available to all his people'.

CHAPTER ONE

Crisis

There is a truth about us and for us in our pain. We may not immediately understand what our pain is trying to tell us, but we can be assured it is nudging us towards change. This is especially true in moments of crisis, where the pain becomes so intense that it catapults us towards change. Our illusions are wiped away as the truth begins to assert itself. It is painful because we have to recognise that the foundations we once built our world on were shifting sand.

It is this human, painful experience of crisis that I have chosen as the point of entry for understanding the spirituality of St Francis de Sales. Whilst it does not mark the beginning of his spiritual life, it does point to an important stage in the process of his spiritual maturation. It is in this crucible of suffering that Francis' spirituality matures.

In short, Francis is exposed to a doctrine of predestination which is at odds with his understanding of God as love. Unable to reconcile these two opposing ideas, Francis succumbs to a type of despair and believes himself lost. The pain he endures is a product of this erroneous thinking. Since it was not a true understanding of God it only succeeded in enslaving Francis, alienating him from God and, indeed, from his true self. Thus, the suffering that Francis undergoes purifies him and leads him to the truth. The pain invites him to change. It is the tilling of his being, the blade that runs through and ploughs up his being, preparing the soil for new growth. He can no longer continue in his illusion. Churned up, in the darkness of his pain, new seeds are being planted. He has to await their growth in darkness.

None of us can go throughout life without such moments of

darkness and crisis. The events that cause the darkness may vary, but the darkness is the same. This experience of darkness is at once deeply personal and universal. We may not be able to identify with the cause of Francis' darkness, but we may well relate to his experience of anguish as he wrestles with the darkness. The experience of crisis and darkness, for each of us, is very much a personal experience of the fall where we find ourselves outside the garden, exiled from Eden. However, once the nugget of truth contained in our pain is unearthed, then this breakdown can become a breakthrough.

In this respect, the details of the crisis are not what matters most;[1] rather, it is the truth and meaning which is discovered that is of lasting value. Thus, our explanation of his crisis is an attempt to unearth this treasure hidden therein. It is an attempt to discover the truth *about* Francis and *for* Francis in his pain. This is the prism through which we shall view this early crisis of St Francis de Sales to lay the foundation for his understanding of the spiritual life.

The truth about Francis in his crisis:
Francis, being the eldest of thirteen children, was expected to follow in his father's footsteps and don his father's mantle. Thus, at an early age he is sent to Paris to study philosophy.[2] However, his father did not intend that his son's sojourn in Paris should be spent totally immersed in books in the classroom. This period was intended as important formative years in his career as a courtier and nobleman. He had to learn the art of *civileté*, to present himself suitably in the great houses where the De Sales family had connections and also at court itself. However, while studying philosophy, Francis also attended theology lectures held at the Sorbonne. Reflecting on those days he confides to a friend:

> In Paris, I learnt many things to please my father and theology to please myself.[3]

Under the tutelage of Genebrard, Francis is introduced to an exposé on the Song of Songs which reveals creation as a love story between God and humanity. Francis is swept along by this newly discovered truth and writes how he 'delights in the charms of God, becomes intoxicated with God and longs to dwell in the beloved tents of God's virtue'. It is a highly idealistic portrayal of himself in relation to God and contains all the excessiveness of a newly discovered love. This stage of infatuation continues for a while until the 'reality' of the adolescent Francis bursts the 'romantic' bubble. As well as the ideal he cherishes, he 'discovers in himself a new man, or rather he was becoming a man according to nature, and the reality of the flesh shocked his fine ideal, the ideal of virginity for the love of Christ'.[4]

This tension between his youthful idealism and adolescent reality, between the religious values in his humanistic studies and the secular values proffered by the ancient philosophers, serve to throw him into crisis. Unable to reach the ideal he has set himself, he now swings from the heights of being in love with God to the depth of despair, where he imagines himself lost:

> He fell prey to great temptation, says Saint Chantal, and to extreme distress of mind. He felt absolutely that he was damned, and that there was no salvation for him, and this paralyzed him.[5]

The core of the crisis was predestination. The possibility that he might not be among the chosen and, therefore, separated from the God he loved above all else. This threw him into the deepest depression which lasted six weeks, from December 1586 until January 1587.

He finally overcame this temptation through an act of faith. He entered the Dominican church of Saint-Etienne-des-Grès, as he was accustomed to doing. In the chapel of the Black Virgin, he made an heroic act of abandonment. He then recited the memorare. As Jane de Chantal testifies, 'he felt as if the illness had fallen to the ground like the scales of a leper'. He found himself immediately cured. This resolution is not in the direction of certainty. The doubt remains – he still does not know if he is among the saved, but the focus has shifted from self to God. This shift brings a purified hope which relies not on his own merits, but on the mercy and goodness of God. He has moved in the direction of *Pure Love*, a love that loves God for himself. Thus, in Paris, is laid the foundation on which Francis will build his theological optimism.

Different commentators vary in their assessment of this pivotal experience in the life of St Francis de Sales. Some understand it from a purely psychological perspective, that Francis' scrupulous nature gets the upperhand whenever his superhuman ideal clashes with his adolescent reality. A combination of overwork, the pessimistic theological milieu, and his own sensitive temperament lead him to experience existentially a theology of despair. This emphasis on the 'negative' within theology only served to compound his sense of shame and accelerated his crisis.

Other commentators understand this crisis from a spiritual perspective, likening it to the mystical experience of the dark night of the soul.[6] They argue that the adult Francis, when talking about this period of his life, often refers to it as a temptation to despair, a spiritual trial. However, they fail to recognise that after the experience, Francis' prayer life is still of a discursive nature.[7] It would seem that both of these positions are extreme and that it cannot be minimised to a period of depression nor exalted to the dark night of the soul. Whether it was mystical or not is debatable, but what is certain is that this experience reached the deepest strata of his spirit and left an indelible impression.

The truth about Francis is that this crisis is unresolved. This initial crisis of 1587 lasts only a few weeks, but the problem continues to haunt his spirit. As Liuima points out, in 1591, 1594, 1596, the question returns:

God does not make you fail, if you do not make yourself fail.[8]

The crisis Francis experiences at Paris, resurfaces five years later at Padua. It is a complex crisis confronting him at several emotional and intellectual levels. Above all it is a crisis of conscience.

His difficultly lies in reconciling St Thomas' and St Augustine's thoughts on predestination with his own.[9] He defends the freedom of God, human freedom, divine mercy and divine justice. What he rejects absolutely is that God would will the sinner and his sin in order to demonstrate his justice. However, to turn his back on these two doctors of the church threw him into utter confusion.[10] Nevertheless, he could not deny what was obvious to him nor accept an opinion which went against human experience.

Having decided to respectfully set aside the teaching of St Thomas and St Augustine, Francis is anything but triumphant. He has agonised over this, but feels obligated to state the truth as he sees it. He is not motivated by pride to take this 'independent' position; on the contrary, he will willingly sacrifice his position, and exchange all knowledge 'in order to know Christ'.[11] He cannot accept the Thomist position because it seems contrary to the salvific will of God as expressed in Christ. God desires to save everyone. Having wrestled with the Thomist opinion and his own conscience, he takes comfort in the following answer:

> I do not will the death of the sinner, but rather that he be converted and live ... I have made you like all other things for myself. My will is nothing other than your sanctification, and my soul hates nothing that it has made.[12]

The issue is resolved by rejecting any teaching that turns God into a self-righteous tyrant. Instead, Francis accepts unreservedly the God revealed by Jesus, a God of mercy and love.[13]

The truth for Francis in his crisis

> We have places in our heart which do not yet exist, and into them enters suffering, in order that they may may have existence. (Léon Bloy)

Francis gives testimony to the accuracy of this statement. His heart is expanded through this on-going crisis and he emerges convinced of the infinite love of God. When he will later talk about the mysteries of God's love, he will do so from his experience:

It is not until the crisis that his soul centres on the love of God. He is absorbed in this single idea to such an extent that his whole life is nothing else than a continual growing and progress in the love of God. Just as charity towards the poor characterized the life of St Vincent de Paul, and charity towards the sick St Camillus de Lellis, so too, with Francis, it is the love of God that characterizes his life.[14]

It was not only the heart of Francis that was affected and moulded by this crisis, but his whole intellectual and theological outlook was given a definite form. Years later, in his *Treatise On the Love of God*, we can see the residual effects of the experience he underwent in his student days at Paris:

'Perfect charity casts out fear.' Yes, in all truth it does so, Theotimus, for fear of being damned and fear of losing paradise are dreadful and full of anguish. How then could they remain in the company of sacred love, which is all sweet and all pleasing?[15]

Emerging from the trauma of this temptation, Francis is convinced of God's desire to save all mankind. He gathers biblical texts, and especially gospel texts, which affirm that the will of God is to save all:

'Before the face of all peoples, a light of revelation to the gentiles, and to the glory of Israel', that divine goodness does not will 'that any should perish', but 'that all should come to the knowledge of the truth', and that 'he wishes all mankind to be saved'.[16]

Having passed through the crucible of suffering, where he is led to the brink of despair, his vision of God is one that will celebrate the immensity of God's love. He, thus, chooses a form of predestination that does not exclude anyone, but acknowledges that we are predestined to happiness, to become the adopted children of God. Predestination, therefore, is the Father's loving plan for us all. The nugget of truth that he has mined from the core of his being, having journeyed through the darkness, is that God desires to save everyone. This desire manifests itself concretely in God's 'active' involvement in salvation history.

This affirmation that God desires to save all is the fundamental truth for Francis that he gleans from this crisis experience. There are other truths that he discovers which we will examine shortly, but this remains the cornerstone. It is the foundation on which his spirituality is built. Everything is to be understood in terms of God's providence, God's desire to save everyone. Thus, his distinction between natural and supernatural providence, or anthropology and revelation, is only a nuancing of the one truth that God desires to save everyone. Both our human nature and our supernatural nature, as revealed by Christ, attest to the single reality that we are the creation of a loving God.

Another personal truth for Francis, gleaned from his crisis and relevant to all our spiritual journeys, is the movement away from self-love to genuine love of God. This he describes as *Pure Love*. His first crisis at Paris is a purification. He is in love with the idea of being in love with God, carried along by a very affective piety. It is the stage of infatuation which yet has to be tested. As such, it is 'too much on the side of excitement and enthusiasm and too little on the side of that quiet, thoughtful, respectful presence St John of the Cross would call contemplation'.[17] As Francis himself writes, 'we are more in love with the consolations of God than the God of consolations',[18] if we don't remain faithful in the midst of trials and tribulations. What Francis acknowledges is that there is a journey to be made from infatuation to real love. We have to pass through the pain of separation, where our idealised romantic love collapses, and we move from being in love to truly loving the other.

The crisis sets Francis on the path, then, of pure love – a love which is 'disinterested' in the sense that it seeks nothing for itself, but only to respond in love to God. We can see this clearly in the prayer he formulates during his crisis:

Whatever may happen, O God, you who hold all things in your hand, whose ways are justice and truth, whatsoever you may have decreed concerning me in the eternal secret of your predestination and reprobation, you whose judgments are unfathomable, you who are ever Just Judge and Merciful

Father, I will love you always, O Lord, at least in this life! At
least in this life will I love you, if it is not given me to love you
in eternity! ... If my merits demand it, and I am to be one
damned among the damned ... grant that I should not be
among those who curse your name.[19]

The major shift for Francis, from this experience, is that he is no
longer at the centre. This resolution is not in the direction of certainty. The doubt remains, he still does not know if he is among
the saved, but the focus has shifted from self to God. This shift
brings a purified hope which relies not on his own merits, but on
the mercy and goodness of God. He has moved in the direction
of *Pure Love*, a love that loves God for God alone.[20]

Two things are worthy of note here. Firstly, pure love does
not depend on feelings but is an act of the will; and secondly, the
purified hope it gives birth to does not depend on our merits but
on God's goodness. Let us examine these two truths for Francis.

In the throes of his crisis at Paris, Francis chooses to love God
even though he has no guarantee of what will happen to himself. One could say that in 'Paris he conceived *pure love* existentially', whereas in Padua 'he fully realised intellectually what it
was'.[21] He realises that the submission of one's will, in imitation
of Jesus in the garden of Olives, is the summit of pure love. Such
a response can only be done out of pure love, and this emerges
from the supreme point of our spirit, where it is unfelt and unseen.
It is not a question of feeling but of faith. This is not a romantic
love that we are talking about. It is a heroic love based on
perseverance and sacrifice for the beloved. Jesus, in the agony in
the garden, is our model in this regard, 'not my will be done, but
thine' (Mk 14:36).

To love, then, is an act of will, an act of resignation where we
choose the will of God. Mary imitates Jesus perfectly in this regard, 'let what you have said be done to me' (Lk 1:38). Here we
have the reversal of our original rebellion when through our
first parents we exercised the freedom of our will over and
against God's will for us. Jesus, the new Adam, reverses the pat-
tern of the Fall by living in perfect unity with God's will for him.

This notion that the love of God does not reside in good feelings, but in conformity with the will of God, is the hub of Salesian spirituality. Francis knows this from experience. When, in Padua, five years after the Paris crisis, he still senses his unworthiness because he remembers 'the sins and imperfections caused by the company he had kept'. It is not his feelings of 'unworthiness' that dictate his response, but rather his hope in the mercy and goodness of God. Continually in his letters of spiritual direction, he will encourage people to have trust and confidence in the goodness of God. This is the foundation of his hope and explains why Salesian spirituality is rooted in optimism. As Lajeuine writes:

> Pure hope, founded on God's mercy alone, is a corollary of pure love, the love that loves God for himself and the universe in God. In Paris, grace laid the foundation on which Francis would build his theological optimism in Padua.[22]

Not only does Francis emerge from his crisis with a purified love, but also with a purified hope. It is a hope not based on the worthiness of human nature, but on the goodness of God.

CHAPTER TWO

The Human Heart

He made us, we belong to Him. (Ps 99)

We are good because God, who has created us, is good. Being a Christian humanist, Francis recognises that we are created good because God, the Creator, is good.[1] It follows that in our very human nature there is an attraction towards the good, towards God who is goodness itself. He writes:

> As soon as we give a little attentive thought to God, we feel a certain sweet emotion within our heart ... and this testifies that God is God of the human heart ... This pleasure, this confidence that our heart naturally has in God, assuredly comes from nowhere but the congruity existing between God's goodness and our soul.[2]

Our heart is made in such a way that we long for what is good, beautiful, and true. This longing is for God. Reflecting on our own experience, our own desires reveal this very longing. Everyone is marked with this longing. Francis adds:

> The human heart inclines towards God, naturally, without knowing really who he is, but when he finds him at the source of faith, he sees him so good, so beautiful, so gentle, so kind to all and so eager to give himself to all who want him.[3]

The humanism of Francis de Sales is one that inevitably leads to the love of God. As Kelley writes, 'He teaches us to penetrate beneath the surface and there will be found a humanism, but one that is divine, one directed by and towards God. Behold man or woman and you behold a creation but God according to his own likeness; love divine beauty and you will also be loving, not only the good, but God himself'.[4]

Francis repeats again and again that there is a *correspondence*, a mutual suitability, between God and the human person, who is made in the image and likeness of God. Out of our need, we go in search of God who has already gone in search of us, to satisfy and fill us with his love. Even of God it is true to say 'it is more blessed to give than receive'. God loves to give. We are poor, God is rich. We need the good, God wants to give what is good to us. We are empty, God is rich in mercy and loving-kindness. Our poverty, lack, corresponds to God's wealth, fullness. Thus, this situation of *our need* and *God's desire to give and respond to our need* is described by Francis as a sweet and desirable meeting:

> There is an unparalleled correspondence between God and man because of their reciprocal perfection. This does not mean that God can receive any perfection from man. But just as man cannot be perfected except by divine goodness, so also divine goodness can rightly exercise its perfection outside itself nowhere so well as upon our humanity. The one has great need and capacity to receive good; the other has great abundance and great inclination to bestow it.[5]

THE HUMAN HEART: THE PARADISE OF GOD

Divine unity has been responsible for the goodness and the beauty of the universe. In effect, all has been ordained by God. But what specially strikes Francis in this world produced by God, is the human person, 'the perfection of the universe … be holy because I am holy; let him who is holy be yet more sanctified and he who is just, let him be still more justified; be perfect as your heavenly Father is perfect' (Mt 5).

> The human person is the perfection of the universe, the mind is the perfection of the human person, love that of the mind, charity that of love. That is why the love of God is the end, the perfection and excellence of the universe.[6]

Francis can talk about the person as being the perfection of the universe, as he says that God exercises his love in creation, but nowhere as perfectly as in the human person. Indeed, Francis describes the human person as 'the paradise of paradises'. Just as the earthly paradise was made to be our dwelling place so too we were made to be 'the dwelling place of God'. This is a recurrent motif with Francis, 'God made your heart for his paradise'.[7]

For Francis, the human person is God's unique masterpiece, the 'human person is the axis of the universe'. We are God's work of art:

> When God, with his almighty hand, formed the human person out of the slime of the earth … it would be a body without movement, without life and without beauty until God breathed into it 'the breath of life', that is holy charity.[8]

First of all, Francis recognises that we are created from the 'slime of the earth'. There is a lowliness within us, we are of the earth. Francis will continually return to this in his letters of spiritual direction, because he will remind us that we are not angels, that God did not create us as angels and it is wrong for us to try and act like angels![9] 'God saves us and sanctifies us in and through our humanness.' We must take our body into account. This is the way God has created us.

> Charity obliges us to love our body fittingly insofar as it is necessary in order to do good. It is part of our person and it will share in our divine happiness. The Christian should love his own body as a living image of the body of the incarnate Saviour, as a branch from the same trunk, and consequently, related to him by affinity and consanguinity.[10]

However, as Francis notes, this body of ours would be without 'movement', 'life' and 'beauty' if God had not 'breathed into it'. What is this breath? Francis goes on to describe it as love. This is the great affinity between us and God – love. This is the mark of the divine within us. This is *the* sign that we are created by God who is love. Thus, just as God is perfect in love, we too are called to love:

> In us all things must be set in order by love and for love.[11]

This, then, is our universal calling to holiness, everyone is called

to love. It is in and through our love of God and neighbour that
we give glory to the God who has created us:

> Let us be what we are and be that well, in order to bring hon-
> our to the Master Craftsman whose handiwork we are.[12]

It is love which constitutes God as God, and thus, as humans, we
most realise the image of divine life within us when we love.
According to Francis, love is the measure and meaning of humanity.[13] Love enters into the very make-up of our humanity,
into the innermost structure of our being. It is love that defines
us as human.[14] Created out of love we are made for love. Thus
our ability to love reflects the Creator who has created us. As
André Ravier points out, 'the heart of God has made the human
heart'.[15] The heart is the central point of meeting between God
and humankind. It is in the *supreme point* of the spirit wherein
we discover our *imago Dei*.[16]

It is not surprising, then, that if love is our calling the heart
should feature so prominently in the writings of St Francis de
Sales to describe both our love and the love of God.

THE HUMAN HEART: THE TEMPLE OF GOD

The human heart is at the centre of our being. It is the place that
encloses the mystery of our being, for God resides there in a special way. To help us understand this mysterious reality of our
personhood, Francis has recourse to the image of the Jewish
temple. To indicate the sacredness of this supreme point of our
spirit he compares it to the inner sanctuary of the temple wherein
no-one was allowed to enter except the High Priest; the only
light permitted was through the door as there were no windows.
Just as the inner sanctuary is the place where God dwells more
particularly, so too the supreme point of our spirit is the place
where the *imago Dei* is fully expressed. As Francis himself says:

> Our soul, in so far as it is reasonable, is the true temple of the
> great God and he dwells there in a most special manner.[17]

In his letters to Philothea in *An Introduction to the Devout Life*, he
had already written:

> 'Wherever we are, we find God present', but we do not think

of it; so we must 'challenge our souls to an attentive consideration of his presence'. God is not only present in the place
where you are, Philothea, but 'most especially in your heart',
'like the heart of your heart, your soul is the temple of God.
In this temple, with holy moments of recollection, brief but
fervent, perceptible to God alone, come and find him, in the
midst of our labours and cares, to adore him, to love him, to
bless him, to invoke him with secret "aspirations, spontan-
eous prayers and good thoughts".'[18]

Just as it was necessary to pass through a series of outside courts
to reach the inner sanctuary of the holy of holies, so too with the
human person we need to pass through the outer tabernacle of
our body to the inner tabernacle of our soul or heart. Within our
heart, then, is another series of 'courts' we need to pass through
in order to reach the supreme point of our spirit.[19] This is our
inner sanctuary, our holy of holies.

In order to reach the supreme point of our spirit, the inner
sanctuary of our holy of holies, we need to pass through different levels of consciousness. It is by making this inner journey
that we enter into our own inner sanctuary and become the high
priest of our being. This journey into the supreme point of our
heart is not to isolate us from others; on the contrary, by exercis-
ing our priesthood in the depths of our being, we reach the
source of the living waters of faith, hope and charity. These naturally lead us out into service of others. Here we discover our
vocation is love.

Made in the image of God, the *raison d'être* of our being is to
love:

> Love is the life of the heart. Just as weight gives movement to
> the moveable parts of a clock, so love gives to the soul what-
> ever movement it has.[20]

The seat of love, then, is the heart. The human heart expresses
what is central to human nature and how it resembles the divinity:

> The heart refers, as it does in the Bible, to that which is most
> profound, inalienable, personal and divine in us; it is the

mysterious centre where each person meets God, responds to his call or refines it.[21]

It is true that the rest of creation bears the traces of 'God's footprints'[22] but only humanity is made in the image of God. This likeness is especially visible in the human heart. However, Francis also acknowledges the paradox that while it is our heart that most resembles God, it is still only a pale reflection of the infinite love of God:

No Theotimus, we can never comprehend (God) for, as St John says, 'He is greater than our heart'.[23]

Nevertheless, God is 'God of the human heart'.[24]

God does not leave us without resources, even as regards nature, to raise ourselves to God. Our effort, our human effort is necessary, and this effort is neither impossible nor vain:

Since God wills to provide people with the natural means necessary for them to render glory to his divine goodness, he has produced on their behalf all other animals and plants … a variety of lands, seasons, waters, winds and rains … the elements, the sky and the stars.

In spite of the many ways in which God generously provides for us, Francis is realistic enough to acknowledge that our response can often be lacking. We can resist and even turn away. However, despite our disobedience, Francis remains firmly convinced that despite 'the Fall' human nature, although tainted, is essentially good. We are naturally attracted towards the good, and it follows that we are naturally attracted towards God who is the supreme goodness. However, because of the Fall, our will is attracted towards what we perceive to be good, but sometimes what we perceive to be good does not turn out to be *the* good.[25]

THE HUMAN HEART: A PRODIGAL HEART

Francis offers us many images to convey this truth of our heart that turns away from *the good* and goes off in search of a perceived good. One of the stories that illustrates this perfectly is that of the baby partridge:

Among partridges it often happens that certain of them steal

the eggs of others so that they may hatch them out. As soon
as the partridge that was hatched out and nourished under
the wings of the strange hen hears the first call of its true
mother, it returns to her ... and so it is with our heart.[26]

God is like our real mother. Our heart is asleep because it has been
nourished under the wings of our surface desires. However,
when these fail to satisfy us, our longing opens us up to hearing
the cry of our real mother. And so our prodigal heart begins its
movement back home. Our heart has this capacity to hear the call
of God, though often it is a still, small voice which has to compete
with the other noisy voices that demand our attention.

Although our heart may be fashioned, nourished, and
brought up among corporeal, base, and transitory things,
and so to speak under nature's wings, yet at the first glance it
casts on God, at the first knowledge that it gets of him, that
natural and initial inclination to love God, which was as
though drowsy and imperceptible, awakens in an instant.
Suddenly it appears like a spark from among the ashes. It
touches our will and gives to it a glow of that supreme love
owed to the sovereign and first principle of all things.[27]

What Francis clearly acknowledges is the fact that our 'prodigal
heart' can lead us on a journey away from our true self, the core
of our being. This happens because there are 'two portions' in
our soul or heart. The inferior and the superior: the inferior relies on the 'experience of the senses' and the superior is in rap-
port with 'the judgment of the spirit'. This distinction between
the two parts of the soul is very pacifying. Our 'bad' nature is
not our real personality.[28] Francis remains confident despite our
sins. If we were delivered too quickly from our difficulties, we
might become presumptuous. This is why he recommends
patience with everyone, but especially, with oneself. He even
says that God allows these 'falls so that we might keep a firmer
grip on his mighty hand'.[29]

It follows that the will can find itself drawn to different attractions and, therefore, drawn two ways at the one time until it
chooses one or the other.[30] In one of his letters he writes:

You are right when you say there are two women in you … there are two daughters of different mothers fighting each other … watch out for this other self … when she happens to attack you suddenly, even if she causes you to totter and stumble, don't be upset; instead call out to Our Lord and Our Lady, they will reach out a blessed helping hand to you, and if they allow you to go on suffering for a while, it will only be in order to have you cry out again more loudly for their help.[31]

Francis identifies the struggle within our own will as captured by Paul, 'I do the things I don't want to, and I don't do the things I want to.'[32] It's not about mastering our will, but rather surrender. Recognising our inability to do anything without God's grace, and relying on God's power, not ourselves.

Experimental union with God simply means putting on the new 'person', 'and this new life is a lively, living and life-giving life'. It is the person who gains this who is able to say: I live now, not I, but God lives in me. 'But whosoever would attain the new life, must make his way by the death of the old.'[33]

Although we have the natural inclination to love God above all things, it is not developed in everybody. It may be enough to get us started, but we find ourselves unable to continue. Put simply, we have the inclination but not the *power* to love God above all things. This instinct, desire, inclination far outstrips our capacity. We're held back by our human condition. It follows that although we can know that God is worthy of love, our will is so feeble that it cannot respond as it should. Sin renders our movement towards union with God impossible, unless we are aided by God's grace. We cannot proceed without God's help, grace is needed. And yet 'it is not without purpose that we have this inclination to love God above all things … that it dwells in our hearts. On God's part, it serves as a crook by which he can gently hold us and draw us to himself.'[34]

Although Francis acknowledges that sin disfigures the image of God in us, it is never entirely destroyed. Even sin has been unable to destroy 'the natural inclination in us to love God above all things'.[35] If the image of God is disfigured in us, then we need to work to restore it. Such a labour of 'love produces zeal' that aims at 'taking away, removing and diverting anything opposed to the beloved object'.[36]

It is now clear that although we have this capacity to love God, we often manage only to produce certain beginnings but find it difficult to advance and be faithful. Our will, as St Paul reminds us, is unable to be strong enough, unaided:

> To wish is within my power, but I do not find the strength to accomplish what is good.[37]

If this is the case, is it not unfair? Is God teasing us to give us a natural inclination to love God above all things, but then we discover that we cannot respond without help? 'Does not nature act in vain when it arouses us to a love that it cannot give to us?' Once again it is the same plight as the woman in the *Song of Songs* who goes out in search of her beloved:

> Love for the beloved had aroused her desire in her, and that desire brought forth an ardour to pursue it. That ardour caused in her a languor that would have annihilated and consumed her poor heart if she had no hope of at length meeting what she sought for.[38]

If God implants in us a desire for the good, for love, for union with him, then it would most certainly be a cause of despair if this desire could not be fulfilled. Such a 'useless desire would be a continued martyrdom for our heart'.[39] But this longing cannot be in vain. It is planted there by God for a purpose. If we manage to be faithful in quite little things, God will not deny his help:

> For though by our sole natural inclination we cannot enjoy the privilege of loving God sufficiently, nevertheless, if we faithfully use this inclination, the sweetness of the devotion to God would help us somewhat and thus we would progress still further. If we conform to this original aid, God's paternal kindness would give us more aid and lead us to do better and better until we reach the highest love to which our natural disposition inclines us; it is indeed a certainty that God's goodness never denies his help for progress to him who does all he can and is faithful in small things.[40]

It is faith which allows us to see that God is the origin, the source of our longing. Thus, although we all have this longing for the good, the beautiful, the true, it does not follow that when we experience them we necessarily conclude that this is God. We need the gift of faith to arrive at this conclusion. Nevertheless, Francis states that at a very human, natural level there is this longing within us. Our nature is already graced by this natural longing. Francis continues, this inclination is a mark, a sign of the secret that we belong to God. Just as a king sets stags and deers free to roam in the forest, but still bearing his coat of arms on their collars, we too are marked with this longing.

The key thing for Francis, however, is that our will is attracted towards the good. This is the way God has made us. And although we cannot now simply depend on our human nature to arrive at this goal, God gives us an extra hand through his grace, as our human nature, through Christ, has been raised to a new level. Francis proceeds to make the distinction between natural and supernatural providence. When we discover our natural inclination towards the good, beautiful and true, we find that this is maybe enough to get us started but not to keep us going. It's at this point that grace comes into play if we co-operate with God's gift.

CHAPTER THREE

The Heart of God

Your heart, O God, is restless, until we rest in you.

(Von Balthasar)

St Augustine has said that the human heart is restless and will not be at rest, until it rests in God. Von Balthasar reworks this Augustinian dictum, which vividly captures the Salesian notion of God's restless heart for us. Why is God's heart restless? Because God is love, and love goes in search of the beloved. Understanding the dynamics of love helps us to appreciate the 'restlessness' of God's heart for us. Francis came to appreciate this fundamental truth when attending lectures on the *Song of Songs* given by the Benedictine, Gilbert Genebrard. In his commentary Genebrard interprets the drama of the lover and the beloved as the unfolding of God's love story with creation.[1] Indeed, Francis himself, in one of his last Christmas sermons, speaks of creation as the first visitation of God's love and the incarnation as being the second visitation of God's love.[2] It is the same logic at work. Love alone is the hermeneutical key that unlocks the mystery of creation and the incarnation. Both reveal the loving heart of God.

A LOVE WHICH CREATES AND PROVIDES

For Francis, the vestiges of God are to be found everywhere in created reality, 'for God has impressed upon all created things his traces, signs of passage and footsteps'.[3] A profound beauty and harmony permeates creation which leads us to contemplate the author behind the masterpiece.

The idea of creation as an act of love on the part of God is familiar to most of us. What is not so familiar is the Salesian conviction that this act of love continues and is itself the world's preservation. The originality of Salesian theology emphasises the eternal present of the creative force of God's love. God is the intimate love of all that is, and the act of creation, far from taking place in the distant past, is taking place continually. God is viewed as one single 'act', hence emphasising the continuous nature of creation and God's involvement in the story of salvation:

> God is one sole, most supremely unique and most uniquely supreme perfection and this perfection is one sole, most purely simple and most simply pure act. Since it is simply the divine essence itself, it is therefore always permanent and eternal.[4]

When Francis talks about creation, he is talking about a dynamic reality. It is not something in the past, it is an ever-present reality. God just didn't create and let things go on like a clock that's been wound up. No, for Francis, creation is continuous, it is happening now, God continues to create. This will be very important when we talk explicitly about Salesian prayer. For the moment, just note that creation is something that is happening now. God is constantly creating and speaking ceaselessly through creation. Not only does God create but Francis adds, 'God also preserves, governs, redeems, saves and glorifies all people in general and each person in particular.'[5]

The God that Francis is talking about here is the God of the Bible, the God who is with us, who accompanies us, who journeys with us. It is the God revealed to Moses, 'I am who am' (Ex 3:14), who is active, dynamic, which means, I am the one who will be with you. Here we get to the kernel, the essence of what Francis is saying about God. God is the one who journeys with us, is our companion, is active in our lives. The emphasis is on movement, on activity, on being with.

Why this activity, this movement on the part of God? Because God is love, and love expresses itself in movement, activity, in doing the loving thing. As Francis says: God's love is a movement, or at least an active habit tending to movement.[6]

This continual creative act of God because of God's love, emphasises God's involvement in the story of our salvation. Love, then, is not a property of God. It is not something God has, nor is love something which God can decide to give here and withhold there. It is not 'love' in the sense of sentiment or passing fancy, but a deep inbuilt disposition to charity which does not change through time. Thus, when Francis describes God's love as an 'activity' or 'movement' he is describing a way of being. God's love is a movement which actively involves him in our lives, culminating in the gift of his only Son.

One of the theological conclusions we can draw from this idea of the permanent creation of the universe, is that God is active, involved in our world. Hence, as Francis writes, 'we speak of God, not so much according to what he is in himself, but rather according to his works'.[7] Thus, there is no distinction between creation and providence because the God that brings into being is also the God who sustains.[8] God is not only involved, God is passionately involved. The divine will is not some passive desire on God's part, rather it is conceived by Francis as 'an active, fruitful, fertile action that excites, invites and urges'.[9]

Francis does not shy away from the darker aspects of reality which would seem to negate the fact that everything is guided by the loving design of God. He argues that if our finite minds were able to understand the *why*, then it would not say much for God's infinity.[10] 'Death, affliction, sweat, and toil ... poverty, hunger, thirst, sorrow, sickness, persecution'[11] when looked at 'apart from God's will are naturally bitter'.[12] However, we are unable to see them from God's point of view. It is only in trusting in the providence of God that we can see that 'they have a place in the world like shadows in a picture which give grace to it and seem to lighten up the painting'.[13]

The image of the Creator-Provider God that emerges from his *Treatise* is one which certainly differs from a blind order. 'There is nothing blind or impersonal in this providence. It is a love living in a heart, a heart which on earth used to beat in the Man-God and mystically continues to beat in heaven.'[14] Indeed, it is to be noted that when speaking of divine providence, Francis frequently personifies God and depicts God as a loving parent, as in the following letter to one of his directees:

> He has watched you till now. All you have to do is to keep a tight hold on the hand of providence and God will help you in all that happens and where you cannot walk he will carry you in his arms ... what can a child fear in the arms of such a Father?[15]

God's providential love is a love which not only brings into existence (creation), but continues to sustain, nourish, accompany (providence) that which he has created.

A LOVE THAT DESIRES TO COMMUNICATE

It follows naturally from the above considerations that an active God, a God of continuous *movement*, should also be a God that desires to communicate with us:

> From all eternity there is in God an essential communication by which the Father, in producing the Son, communicates his entire infinite and indivisible divinity to the Son. The Father and the Son together, in producing the Holy Spirit, communicate in like manner their own proper unique divinity to him.[16]

As Lajeunie says 'it is *communicative* love, from which creation sprang, from which the Incarnate Word came to us, from whom we receive with no finite limits all the graces of life.'[17] God is communicative and this is constitutive of the three persons within God. However, it is this same communicative essence which causes God to go 'outside' to create.[18] The explosion of love within God desires to communicate itself *ad extra*:

> God made his dwelling in himself. His centre was no other than himself. Also when he desired to communicate himself to man he went out of himself: he made, as it were, an effort. He had been ... in a state of rapture and ecstasy by which he went out of himself in order to communicate with his creature.[19]

God's movement outward is in response to our restlessness of heart.[20] He desires to fulfill our deepest longings. Thus, not only 'can he communicate himself to us, but he will do so'.[21] Francis re-enacts this drama between the all-loving God and the soul that thirsts for him, relying heavily on the *Canticle of Canticles*. He describes God as being *jealous* for our friendship,[22] not in the sense of concupiscence because our love can add nothing to God, but rather a jealousy which is motivated by his pure love and desire to give himself to us:

> Theotimus, I ask you to consider briefly how delicately this divine lover expresses the nobility and generosity of his jealousy: 'They have forsaken me who am the source of living water', he says. It is as if he said, 'I do not complain that they have forsaken me because of any injury that abandonment by them can bring me … I grieve over their misfortune in that having left me they have been deceived by holes that have no water.'[23]

This allusion to the prophet Jeremiah clearly reveals the altruism of God's love which seeks nothing for itself. Or as Francis continues, 'I look for nothing in their love but their happiness'. Of course it is in the incarnation that God chooses the most perfect way of communicating his love by uniting his nature to human nature.

A LOVE THAT IS ECSTATIC

The nature of God's communication with mankind is ecstatic, in the strict etymological sense of the word, that is, he goes out of himself as it were to share his divine nature with human beings.[24] It is a movement from love, to love, in love.[25] This sharing is the essence of Francis's mysticism which we may call the *ecstatic love* of God:[26]

> He has been in ecstasy. As St Dionysus says, this is not only because by his excessive love he goes in a certain manner outside himself, and thus extends his providence to all things and is in all things. It is also because, as St Paul says, in some manner he has forsaken himself, he has emptied himself …

> he has 'annihilated himself' to come down to our humanity
> to fill us with his divinity ... So greatly has love for mankind
> ravished God and drawn him into ecstasy![27]

In analysing this citation we can clearly see that 'ecstasy' in God
is linked to his 'excessive love'. The ecstatic love of God is not
simply a love which overflows into creation, which is entirely
dependent on his love, but is a love which is pure, emptying itself
of self. Francis explains this through the use of verbs such as
'forsake', 'empty', 'annihilate' which denote the utter selfless-
ness of God's action. There is no self-interest in God's love for us
– it is pure love:

> It is not to God's advantage that we should love him but to
> ours. Our love is useless to him, but to us it brings great profit.
> If it pleases him, it is because it is profitable to us. Since he is
> the supreme good, he takes pleasure in communicating him-
> self by his love, although from it no benefit whatsoever can
> accrue to him.[28]

As has already been established, this quotation affirms that God
'takes pleasure in communicating himself' because he looks for
nothing else but our happiness. Francis distinguishes between
God's pure love and our love. God's love is benevolent, 'since he
wills and makes whatever good there is in us and then takes
complacence in that good'. Our love, on the contrary, 'begins
from our complacence in the supreme goodness and infinite
perfection which we know to be in the divinity, and next we
come to the exercise of benevolence'.[29] The generosity of God
knows no bounds, it is of his nature to give of himself.[30]

The supernatural providence of God in Jesus:
We have already established that Francis regards the divine love
at work in creation and watching over the world as the 'natural
providence of God'. However, he proceeds to distinguish another
level, the 'supernatural providence of God' which is revealed
through the incarnation.[31] In the person of the Son of God made
man, made through his birth of a real human mother 'child of
the human race',[32] God associates humanity with divinity, so

that this humanity can enjoy eternally his infinite glory. It follows that 'the mystery of the incarnation is at the heart of creation'.[33]

In the Salesian perspective, natural providence reveals God's desire that all be saved, the purpose of creation. What natural providence does for all people, supernatural providence does for those believers who have received God's explicit revelation.[34] Not only does supernatural providence reveal in a new way the incredible love of God for us through the incarnation, but it also reveals the real purpose of creation.[35] In his *Treatise*, Francis conveys the mystery of this reality through the use of a simple parable. He explains that the reason why we plant a vine is the fruit it produces. Thus, the vine is creation and the fruit of the vine is Jesus Christ. Hence Christ is first in God's intention and eternal plan.[36] Creation was always for Christ:

> The mystery of the incarnation reunites the mystery of all creation in order to govern it and afterwards to motivate it: 'I have come so that they may have life and have it to the full …' And how can life superabound, if not in and by love? It seems, then, by re-reading the marvelous Salesian pages on the motive of the incarnation, that everything in the world must converge, as it did in the blessed hour of the annunciation, to pierce better the mystery of being Jesus … everything in the universe is ordered to the realisation of a heart capable of God, a heart capable of loving as God loves.[37]

In order to express adequately how the Son and his incarnation are the goal of creation of humanity, Francis gathers together several citations from scripture of which Colossians, Proverbs, and Sirach mark the primacy of Christ over all creatures:

> Thus all things have been made for him who is both God and man, for which reason he is called 'the first-born of every creature' (Col 1:15), 'possessed' by divine majesty 'in the beginning of his ways, before he made anything,' 'created from the beginning before the world' (Rom 1:22; Sir 24:9). 'For in him were created all things … and he is before all creatures, and in him all things hold together. And he is the head of all the church, holding in all things and in all places the first place' (Col 1:16-18).[38]

It is clear from this that Francis adopts the Pauline tradition which gives his concept of love its immense grandeur. 'The union in one person of divinity and creature makes this union the cornerstone of the whole cosmos. The whole cosmos is united to God by this union.'[39]

From all of this emerges the priority of the incarnation of the Son as being wished from eternity and before all things by divine providence, to express outside of himself his essential need to give of himself and thus, make human nature participate in this movement of Trinitarian love. Thus, for Francis, 'the incarnation has a theological priority over creation'.[40] In short, this means that love, not sin, can only explain God's free decision to enter the human race and become one of us.

It is to be remembered that in Salesian thought the incarnation was eternally willed by God.[41] Over and above the fact of the fall, God's eternal plan had destined us for a close companionship with himself. This desire of God to communicate himself is expressed by means of his ecstatic love. The incarnation reveals the ecstatic love, but so too does the coming of the Spirit. Both the incarnation and the coming of the Spirit are prior to the Fall in God's eternal plan:

> With the Salesian notion of the 'eternal coming' of the Spirit, we have an eternal linkage of the missions, even before any consideration of the Fall. With the character of the Spirit linked to the love and heart existing between Father and Son, we can catch some glimpse of the kind of creation that would have existed if the human family had not fallen.[42]

In his last Christmas sermon (1622) he declares:

> The heavenly Father planned the creation of this world for the incarnation of his Son. The end of his work was also the beginning. Divine wisdom saw from all eternity that the eternal Word should assume our nature and come into this world.[43]

Even without original sin, God would have become incarnate in Jesus.[44] The Fall only modifies how God comes to us in Jesus. 'The Son of God comes into the world not as a "homo gloriosus",

a man of glory, but as a sufferer, a man of sorrows.'[45] The incarnate son becomes the Redeemer God: his incarnation will no
longer be only a *gift* of infinite love and goodness, but *pardon* offered by him who, far from finding himself 'overwhelmed' by
the sin, finds himself 'aroused and called forth by it'.[46]

THE INCARNATION AND GOD'S ECSTATIC LOVE FOR MANKIND

Through the incarnation, Jesus comes to restore our portrait to
its original beauty, 'to repay, by means of his death, this image
and likeness of God imprinted in us'.[47] It is in this re-creation
that Francis once again sees the overflowing, ecstatic love of
God:

> Our ruin has been to our advantage since human nature in
> fact has received greater graces by the redemption wrought
> by its Saviour than it would ever have received from Adam's
> innocence even if he had persevered therein.[48]

His thinking is on the same lines as the 'O felix culpa' of
Augustine. However, there is another dimension to be plumbed
in the Salesian understanding of the incarnation. Not only is the
incarnation an historical fact, but also 'a continuous metaphysical and personal fact. It is an event that is perpetually renewed
in the centre of every person … No longer his servants, we are
formed anew as friends by his divine preference'.[49] As Francis
himself says:

> Unless he united himself to us, we would never unite our-
> selves to him. He always chooses us and takes hold of us be-
> fore we choose him or take hold of him. But when we follow
> his imperceptible allurements and then begin to unite our-
> selves to him, he sometimes effects progress in our union. He
> assists our feeble efforts and perceptibly joins himself to us,
> so that we perceive that he has penetrated and entered into
> our heart with incomparable gentleness.[50]

Note how, through the use of verbs like 'unite', 'choose', 'take
hold of', Francis insists on the fact that grace precedes our
response and is always the fruit of the divine initiative. The

redemptive grace of Jesus so strengthens our will that, once again, our natural inclination to love God can be an effective 'crook by which he can gently hold us and draw us to himself'.[51] In this light, the human condition is transfigured. It is converted:

> Just as the rainbow touches the thorn aspalathus and makes it smell sweeter than the lily, so our Saviour's redemption touches our miseries and makes them more beneficial and worthy of love than original innocence could ever have been.[52]

Indeed, in the *Treatise* we see how Francis in the first four books presents Christ as a model to imitate and to follow as the source of life. However, in the fifth book he explains how we have entered into the very death and resurrection of Christ and, therefore, are called to live Christ. Christ is no longer an exterior model; he imprints his mystery in the heart of the lover. Thus, we find in his correspondence to various people that he continually encourages them to 'live Jesus'. This is not just a pious aspiration, but a lived reality.

To symbolise the entry of Christ into the human heart, Francis has recourse to the *Song of Songs* as an expression of God's love for his people.[53] In fact, he writes that not only are we transfigured by the incarnation, but that God the Father cannot but look at us except through the prism of his Son:

> He does not look at us as we are but rather as what we have already become in Christ. God looks at us and desires us.[54]

Thus, the image of God in us takes on christological dimensions. It follows that we are not only in contact with Christ, we are one with him, forming one single 'mystical person' with him:

> Jesus Christ is our love, and our love is the life of our soul. Therefore our 'life is hidden in God with Jesus Christ, and when Jesus Christ who is "our love and therefore our spiritual life", "shall appear" in the day of judgment, we also shall appear "with him in glory". That is, Jesus Christ, our love, will glorify us by communicating to us his own joy and splendour'.[55]

According to Lajeunie, this passage of the *Treatise* prevents us from reproaching Francis with having given an individualistic doctrine on divine love. Francis takes into account the universal dimension of salvation brought and offered by Jesus Christ:

> Salvation is fundamentally a personal adventure but this salvation is made within the church and the social aspect of the drama ought not to be omitted nor diminished. Francis de Sales is very conscious of it and teaches precisely this love which incorporates us all, each and everyone, into Christ, to form the invisible world, hidden in the glory of God.[56]

Here we have the basis of Francis de Sales's mystical christocentrism which is at one and the same time a powerful theocentrism. As Lajeunie states, 'now this life of the Lord is the very life of the Father communicated to the world in order to bring it to its Prime Cause'.[57]

Jesus meek and humble of heart

It is the Matthean Jesus, 'meek and humble of heart' (Mt 11:29), that captures the essence of the Salesian understanding of God's love in Jesus.[58] The desire of God to communicate himself and move out in ecstasy towards us is expressed supremely in the person of Jesus. He embodies the descending movement of God's love when he unites himself to our human nature in the incarnation. He describes the descending movement as follows:

> He poured himself completely into us and, so to speak, dissolved his grandeur so as to reduce it to the form and figure of our littleness. Because of this he is called the fountain of living water, dew or rain *come down* from heaven.[59]

This variation of the Pauline hymn (Phil 2:7) conveys this downward movement, this lowering of self, the humility of Jesus. However, it also reminds us that he humbles himself so that he can exalt us, raise us up to the dignity of children of God. Thus, there is also an ascending movement:

> He divested himself of his grandeur, his glory ... he *annihilated* himself to fill us with his dignity, to fulfil us with his goodness, to raise us up to his dignity and give us the divine being of children of God.[60]

According to Francis, the perfect manifestation of meekness and humility takes place on the cross in Jesus' humble obedience to the will of the Father and his willing forgiveness of his persecutors.[61] It is precisely from the cross that the glory of Christ bursts forth in his humbling of himself.[62]

It is the gentleness of the humble Christ that has the power to arrest our soul and move us to seek his forgiveness. Francis illustrates this by recounting the gospel scene in which the look of Jesus arrests Peter whenever he hears the cock crow:

> The *gentle* redeemer cast a saving look upon him like a dart of love. It pierced that heart of stone which afterwards, like the rock of old struck by Moses in the desert, sent forth so much water.[63]

It is the figure of Jesus crucified that epitomises love's gentleness and humility. It is the supreme expression of the thirst of God in Jesus for our love:

> Our gentle Jesus, who has purchased us with his own blood, infinitely desires us to love him so that we may be saved forever, and he desires us to be saved so that we may love him eternally. His love tends to our salvation and our salvation tends to his love.[64]

In Jesus we see the ecstatic love of God as he surrenders himself to death:

> No man takes my life from me, but I give it up and lay it down of myself; I have the power to lay it down, and I have the power to take it up again (Jn 10:17-18).[65]

This kenotic love of God in Jesus is, above all, passionately involved in our salvation. It is a love which empties itself for the other. It is an active love that seeks the good of the beloved. A love that 'is not content with announcing publicly his extreme desire to be loved, but that goes from door to door knocking' urging us to seek that which we absolutely need in order really to live.[66]

It is through the gentleness and humility of Jesus that God seeks to draw our hearts into his. However, this way of loving which never forces, or else it would not be love, renders God vulnerable. God leaves us free and in that freedom we can choose to reject him as Francis constantly reiterates.[67]

The cross reveals the vulnerability of God's love which is exposed as naked and poor, 'stripped of every affection'.[68] It is a love that loves us to excess. A love that keeps nothing for itself, but pours itself out completely, allowing itself to be stripped completely.[69] This is the embodiment of pure love:

> Let us represent to ourselves, Theotimus, Jesus standing submissively in Pilate's house, where for love of us he was stripped of all his garments one after the other by soldiers, the ministers of his death. Not satisfied with this, they took his very skin from him, tearing it off by blows of their staves and whips. Later his soul was in like manner stripped of its body and his body of its life by the death he endured upon the cross. Love did all this.[70]

In the passage just cited the repetition of the verb 'stripped' and like verbs, 'tearing off', 'taking off', serve to reinforce vividly the utter nakedness of Jesus caused by his immense love. Francis presents Jesus as being literally stripped of his garments and spiritually stripped of any consolations, filled with 'sadness, fear, terror, anguish, abandonment and inner depression such as never had and never shall have an equal'.[71] It is in this nakedness that we see the purity of his love, his total resignation to his Father's will. It follows that there is nothing sentimental about Francis' depiction of love.

There is no way in which Francis' portrayal of the death of Jesus can be misinterpreted to express the will of a despotic god who demands the death of his son as an expiation for sin. The death of Jesus is his 'supreme testimony of his love for the Father'.[72] The son's sacrifice is also the Father's sacrifice of his only son. To emphasise the reciprocal nature of this sacrifice Francis alludes to Abraham's readiness to sacrifice his son:

> O God, who can decide which of these two loves is greater – Abraham's, who to please God sacrifices so loving a child, or that child's who to please God is completely willing to be sacrificed … For my own part, I prefer the Father because of his long suffering, but I also give the prize of greatness to the Son.[73]

There can be no ambiguity. Love alone can explain the death of Jesus. The passion of Christ, like the incarnation itself, is fully involved in the dynamism of the divine goodness seeking to expand itself. According to Francis, the only motive for the passion and death of Jesus is love. Here we find the supreme expression of the pure love of God. Francis conveys this in an original manner by ingeniously linking two comparisons: that of the hard-pressed hart and the dying Christ, to express the supreme abandonment of pure love which can only be understood in terms of the perfect sacrifice of one's life:

> When the hart has lost all breath and is beset by the hounds, gasping out its last sighs and with eyes filled with tears, it throws itself before the huntsman. So when our divine Saviour is near death and sending forth his last breath, with a loud cry and many tears he says, 'Alas, O my Father, into your hands I commend my spirit.' This was the last of all his words, Theotimus, and by it the beloved Son gave supreme testimony to his love for his Father.[74]

The death and cross of Jesus are signs of love 'to the uttermost' (Jn 13:1), they stand out as climax and consummation of the ministry of Jesus in which God's love is embodied. They are the supreme expression of the 'eternal love' of the Father and the Son, a love without equal:

> Consider the eternal love that God has borne towards you. Before our Lord Jesus Christ as man suffered on the cross for you, his divine majesty by his sovereign goodness already foresaw your existence and loved you exceedingly. When did his love for you begin? It began even when he began to be God. When did he begin to be God? Never, for he always has been, without beginning and without end. So also has he always loved you from all eternity.[75]

The outpouring of the love between Father and Son overflows into all created reality. It is through the Son that we have access to the Father. In their exchange of love is unfurled 'the mystical ladder' descending from 'the loving bosom of the eternal Father' and 'planted in the bosom and pierced side of our Saviour'.[76]

In the disfigured person of Jesus hanging on the cross, 'an abyss of beauty',[77] we have the supreme paradox: He who is without beauty reveals true beauty.[78] The source of this beauty is love. Such a beauty can only be seen with contemplative eyes.[79] It is to penetrate an invisible order, the most inexpressible, that of love which has valued the folly of the cross.

The beauty of God, for eternity, will 'shine on the face gloriously sad of him who made himself man'.[80] For Francis, the humanity of Christ will remain eternally the *window* through which God will look at us and through which we will contemplate God:

> See how he makes himself be seen through the wounds of his body and the opening in his side, as through windows and as through a 'lattice which he himself looks out' at us ... To see me more clearly, come to those same windows through which I look at you. Come, look upon my heart in that cleft opening in my side, made when my body, like a house cast down in ruins, was so piteously broken on the tree of the cross![81]

It is through the prism of the wounded heart of Jesus that we may glimpse the excessive love of God for us. And yet, according to Francis, it is not so much that we look at him as him looking at us. His pierced side is the *window* through which the infinite love of God continues to pour itself into our hearts. The death of Christ is, therefore, less an act of justice than a foolish act of love.[82] This is a central idea in Salesian spirituality, as Ravier points out:

> It is from the height of the cross that God, through his Son, throws to us his great call of love. A silent call without words, but urgent. An incontestable call.[83]

CHAPTER FOUR

Prayer: Heart Speaks to Heart

It is obvious from our last chapter that the incarnation highlights the centrality of the human heart in the divine-human drama. Through the incarnation, God reveals his intention to unite human nature to his divinity and he achieves this union through the heart. The human heart and the divine heart unite in Jesus:

> He saw that among all the different ways of communicating himself there was none so excellent as that of joining himself to a created nature in such wise that the creature would be engrafted and implanted in the godhead so as to become with it one single person.[1]

This union of hearts, between God and mankind, is consistently symbolised throughout the *Treatise* by the image of a kiss.[2] It is through this kiss that God draws us to himself and this union will be fully consummated in heaven:

> We will join our will to God to savour and experience the sweetness of his incomprehensible goodness, for at the top of this ladder God bends towards us, gives us the kiss of love, and makes us taste the sacred breasts of his sweetness, which are 'better than wine'.[3]

According to Francis, we can receive presentiments of this 'nuptial kiss' in the present world, because God has invited us to participate in his divine friendship. God is not only God of the human heart but also, 'friend of the human heart'.[4] We are called, then, to seek the divine heart and bring about 'a conformity of our heart to that of God'.[5]

PRAYER IS… GOD'S COMMUNICATION

It is in this context of heart speaking to heart that we can begin to

45

appreciate Francis' understanding of prayer as a dialogue of hearts:

> Prayer is a conversation of the soul with God. If prayer is a conversation then through it we speak to God and God in turn speaks to us. As conversation it is absolutely secret and in it nothing is said between God and the soul if not heart to heart. The language of lovers is so special that no-one can comprehend it except them. Where love reigns there is no need for spoken words or the use of the senses to converse and listen one to the other.[6]

In this dialogue it is always the heart of God that takes the initiative. God's movement outward is in response to our restlessness of heart. He desires to fulfill our deepest longings. Thus, not only 'can he communicate himself to us, but he will do so'.[7] Of course, it is in the incarnation that God chooses the most perfect way of communicating his love by uniting his nature to human nature.

When we begin to understand the movement of love within God, then, the first thing we begin to understand about prayer is that it is not something we do but rather is a *response* to the love of God who is continually drawing us. Francis writes:

> … the soul would not pray unless it were aroused to do so. However, as soon as it is aroused and feels those attractions, it prays that it may be drawn forward. When it is drawn, it runs, but still it would not run if the perfumes that draw, and by which it is actually drawn, did not enliven the heart by the power of their precious odour.[8]

It is only because God, in his love, draws us that we find the strength in our turn to join God. 'No one can come to me unless he is drawn by the Father' (Jn 6:44). This is the meaning of Francis' commentary on the *Song of Songs:*

> Draw me, the sacred Bride tells the one she loves – if I am following you, it is not because you are pulling me but because you attract me. Your attraction is powerful but not violent because its strength is its very sweetness. Perfumes have no other power than their sweetness to draw one after them, and how could sweetness pull if not sweetly and pleasantly.[9]

The only power God exercises over us is his gentleness because 'perfumes have no power to draw us to them except their sweetness'.[10]

It is the 'scent of the divine beloved' that has the capacity to arouse and draw us. This is a scent that 'is poured out' ceaselessly and not dependent on our response. It follows that the perfume of God precedes our response, indicating the unconditional nature of the divine initiative. It also reveals the amazing respect God has for our freedom.

Another image used by Francis to convey God's desire to communicate with us and gently draw us, is the image of breath. This image clearly highlights the role of the Spirit in stirring us to pray. The breath of God blows on 'the sails of our spirit' and 'gives movement to the ship of our heart'.[11]

It is, above all, in the fable of the Apodes[12] that Francis manages to convey in picture form, rather than at a conceptual level, this interplay between God's inspiration and our free response. Citing Aristotle, he tells of the existence of a certain species of birds, Apodes, whose legs are so short and feet so weak that once they land they are unable to take off again. They remain there 'motionless and perish unless a wind favourable to their weakness sends its gusts over the surface of the ground, catches hold of them, and lifts them up'.[13] He traces the delicate way in which this wind encourages and invites the Apodes to risk flight:

> The wind that lifts up the apodes first blows upon their feathers, since they are the lightest parts and most susceptible to its agitation whereby it gives an initial movement to their wings. It spreads them out and unfolds them in such wise as to provide itself with a hold by which to seize the bird and lift it into the air.[14]

It is God who takes the initiative, whose 'breath' as a favourable wind seeks to raise us aloft. However, we can resist this 'gentle force':

> However, if in the same measure as it pushes us forward we push against it so as not to let ourselves go with its movement, then we resist. So also when the wind has seized our

apode birds and raised them aloft, it will not carry them very far unless they spread their wings and co-operate, lifting themselves up and flying through the air into which they have been launched. On the contrary, if they are allured by some green growth they see beneath them, or weakened by their stay on the ground, and instead of responding to the wind keep their wings folded and cast themselves back down on the earth, then they actually received the motion of the wind but to no purpose since they did not avail themselves of it.[15]

The predominant image for the Spirit of God used in this story is that of a gentle wind. Francis speaks of the Spirit as a 'wind which raises our thoughts and pushes our affections into the air of divine love'.[16] At both levels of feeling and thought, God's spirit is active in arousing us to respond in love to God and our neighbour.

Francis describes the inspirations of God's Spirit in the following manner:

By inspirations we mean all those interior attractions, motions, acts of self-reproach and remorse, lights and conceptions that God works in us and predisposes our hearts by his blessings and fatherly love in order to awaken, stimulate, urge and attract us to holy virtues, heavenly love and good resolutions: in short, to everything that sends us on our way to our everlasting welfare.[17]

The fruitfulness of these inspirations of God's Spirit which are always available to us, depends on our consent. There can be no love without freedom:

In spite of the all-powerful strength of God's merciful hand which touches, enfolds and bends the soul with so many inspirations ... grace has the power not to overpower but to entice our hearts.[18]

To the degree we allow our hearts to be 'enlarged and expanded', to the same degree does God 'pour forth his mercy and increasingly spread out holy inspirations'.[19] God ceaselessly seeks our good.

This is eminently true in his inspirations that lead to our prayer of repentance:

> In fact, we would rightly deserve to remain abandoned by God, since by our disloyalty we have thus forsaken him. But his eternal charity does not often permit his justice to impose such chastisement, but rather arouses his compassion and stirs him to rescue us from our misery. He does this by sending out the favouring wind of his most holy inspirations.[20]

If God is provoked by our sinfulness, it is his compassion, more than his justice that is aroused. This compassion is manifested in his inspirations which graciously entice us by their 'gentle force'. It is through such inspirations that the Father draws us to himself. The Father breathes 'sweet allurements' by means of which he draws us to himself; the Son breathes inspirations so as to 'not only knock at the door of the human heart but to call the beloved soul to him'. However, it is the special mission of the Spirit to draw us into the divine life.

The breath within God (the Father and the Son breathe the Spirit) reveals the communication within God, and the breath that emanates from God reveals God's desire to communicate with us. Thus, the Spirit of God communicates through 'inspirations' which arouse us not only to conversion, but set us on the path of union with God. This union expresses itself in a union of hearts. Once again we return to the mystery of the incarnation where a perfect union between the heart of God and humankind takes place in the person of Jesus. Prayer, therefore, is an entering into this mystery where we pray with, in and through Christ.

PRAYER IS ... COMPANIONSHIP WITH GOD

Our creation, according to Francis, is the gift of the trinitarian God who 'chose to create us to have *company* with his Son, to participate in his glory'.[21] When speaking of companionship, Francis often uses the term 'friend' to indicate the intimacy of this relationship between God and humankind. God is not only 'God of the human heart' but also 'friend of the human heart'.[22]

Through prayer we are invited into the friendship that exists within God:

> What is worthy of love and longing if not friendship? If friendship is a thing to be loved and longed for,. whose friendship can be such in comparison with that infinite friendship which obtains between the Father and the Son and together with them, is one and the same most unique God? Theotimus, out of awe for the beauty and sweetness of the love this eternal Father and this incomprehensible Son divinely and eternally exercise, our hearts will themselves be absorbed in love.[23]

The friendship emanating from the divine heart reveals to us that 'God who is sole is not thereby solitary because he is Father and Son in two persons'.[24] This distinction of personhood and yet union of nature is captured by the image of the heart as 'union belongs only to the heart which alone can produce true substantial love'.[25] This friendship of the Father and Son, in turn, is itself another divine person, the Holy Spirit. The Holy Spirit, then, is a 'favourable wind' which lifts up the 'wings of the heart to allow the person to take flight toward the divine'.[26]

It is clear, then, that prayer understood as companionship or friendship with God in Christ, values above all the heart:

> When you prepare to pray you must say with your whole heart and in your heart, 'O my heart, my heart, God is truly there'.[27]

When Francis states that 'we draw God's heart into our own',[28] he emphasises not only the mediative role of the crucified heart of Christ in our relationship with God, but also its transformative role. We quite literally participate in the divine heart by means of Christ's heart because 'love makes lovers equal'.[29] This mystical union is described by Francis as the rhythmic action of two hearts beating as one:

> The Spouse (Christ) pours his love and his soul into the bride's heart and the bride in turn pours her soul into the spouse's heart.[30]

This union leads to a oneness or unity of hearts. A vivid example of such unity is visible, for Francis, in the early Christians where all are said to possess 'one heart', that is the heart of Christ:

> The first Christians were said to have only one heart and one soul because of their perfect mutual love. If St Paul no longer lived for himself but Jesus Christ lived in him, it was because of that most close union of his heart with his Master's, whereby his soul were as if dead in the heart it animated so as to live in the Saviour's heart which it loved. Then, O true God! How much truer is it that the Sacred Virgin and her Son had but one soul, but one heart and but one life.[31]

The pierced heart of Christ is, therefore, the source, means and fulfillment of union. It speaks the silent language of love which prevails over all other language because 'heart talks to heart, and the tongue only talks to the ears'.[32]

The sacraments are to be understood in this prayer context as the interaction of hearts. Since the sacraments lead to union with Jesus they are best understood in terms of the heart.[33] Francis makes use of the image of Jacob's ladder in order to illustrate how the various levels of ascent can bring about this union of hearts. It is in the context of friendship or companionship that the sacraments are to be understood. They are not external rites devoid of warmth and feeling, but rather, the outreach of a loving Christ in his church. Once again the *Song of Songs* best expresses this reality: 'his left arm is under my head and his right embraces me'. This image of loving embrace conveys the reality of the sacraments as Christ, identified with his body the church, who seeks to embrace us.

PRAYER IS ... LIVING JESUS

Prayer, in its essence, is allowing ourselves to be transformed by God into Christ. This is a painful process which strips us of our egoism. Pure love is characterised by abnegation of self as epitomised in Christ's passion. Francis presents Jesus as being literally stripped of his garments and spiritually stripped of any consolations. It is in this nakedness that we see the purity of his love, his total resignation to his Father's will. If prayer is learning to unite our will with the will of God, then the cost must be the cost of Calvary:

> Theotimus, Mount Calvary is the mount of lovers. All love that does not take its origins from the Saviour's passion is foolish and perilous. Love and death are so mingled in the Saviour's passion that we cannot have the one in our hearts without the other.[34]

As in the epilogue of the *Song of Songs*, love is paired with death, bringing us to the culmination of Jesus' stripping where body and soul are divided. Only Jesus on the cross can initiate us into the practice of divine love. This self-emptying through prayer is a painful process, but although we die, we rise to a new life in Christ. Our natural being is reclothed with the beauty of the Son who becomes the *window* through which the Father gazes on us. The essence of Christian prayer, then, is allowing ourselves to die so as to be born again in Christ through whom we have access to the Father.

The authenticity of our prayer is not to be gauged by how we feel. Francis quips that often we are 'more in love with the consolations of God than the God of consolations'.[35] In our journey of prayer there will be moments of aridity, as experienced by Jane Frances de Chantal. Indeed, her aridity was acute, an inner exodus that lasted for more than forty years. We may feel God is absent, but God is always present. St Bernard describes this as a game of divine hide and seek.[36] In line with the Christian tradition, Francis explains that the feeling of withdrawal or absence in prayer is when God is most present, but in an unfelt way. Our hearts are being expanded to receive more of God.

DEGREES OF PRAYER

Prayer, then, for Francis is 'heart speaking to heart'.[37] It is a movement of love between hearts in which the devout heart is united to God and transformed. Francis describes the various degrees of prayer in terms of the heart's response to God's love. He follows closely the degrees of prayer as outlined by St Teresa of Avila:

1. Vocal prayer is 'an overflowing of the heart in words'.[38]
2. Mental prayer is a 'prayer of the heart' that enables us to ruminate on the various aspects of the divine heart.[39]
3. Contemplative prayer allows 'the heart to drink' liquid nourishment which finds its source in the divine heart.[40]
4. Prayer of quiet in which the devout heart rests on the divine heart, as exemplified by John the evangelist resting on the breast of Our Lord at the last supper.[41]

Whilst acknowledging that prayer is above all a gift of God, there are things we can do to make ourselves more open to receiving God's gift of prayer. Francis compares us humorously to a clock that 'no matter how good it may be, it needs resetting and rewinding twice a day, once in the morning and once in the evening.'[42]

In his various recommendations on prayer to different directees, he reiterates the importance of preparation. We are always to put ourselves in God's presence before beginning to pray. This can be done by realising that God is 'in all things and all places'. In particular, it is good to recall that God is especially present in our heart. Following the counsel of St Teresa of Avila, he states that much of our difficulty in prayer comes from believing that God is distant, far away. Thus, like her, he recommends that we imagine Jesus next to us as we would a friend.

Having prepared ourselves in this manner, Francis proceeds to recommend that we select a point or two to meditate on. The scriptures, in particular, offer much that we can ponder on, as they are a word of life and a word for life. We are to be like bees gathering nectar from flowers, we remain with a particular theme drawing whatever benefit we can from it, but then calmly moving on when we can't extract 'any honey from it'.[43] Francis advises us to conclude our period of prayer by thanking God, but also encourages us to choose a point or two from our meditation and to turn back to this 'spiritual bouquet' from time to time during the day:

As birds have their nests as a place to which they retire, and wild animals find safety in their thickets and woods, so our hearts should pick some place each day where they can retire at various times to refresh and renew themselves during their exterior preoccupations. Withdraw from time to time into your own heart, apart from the world, and converse heart to heart with God.[44]

Through reading and meditation, and after talking it over with God in a dialogue of hearts, we are now prepared for a deep enjoyment of God's presence. Thus, meditation gives way to contemplation. Our destiny, the very reason for our creation, is to know, love and contemplate God and his creation for all eternity. This heavenly life, however, must and does begin here and now. We will find it if we but open our hearts to it. Francis compares meditation to eating and contemplation to *drinking*. The first involves effort on our part, the second is pure gift from God. Our longing to gain God's love causes us to meditate; love, when gained, leads to contemplation:

Just like bees sucking the flowers to collect their honey, we meditate to collect the love of God; once it has been collected, we contemplate God and become attentive to his goodness because of the sweetness which love makes us discover there.[45]

In short, Francis says, 'we meditate to awaken love, we contemplate because we love'. Our effort in meditation, then, gives way to God's action as he pours his love into our souls. Our attention is then fixed in a loving regard on God. Contemplation consists, not in thinking much, but in loving much. How do we prepare for contemplation? Since it is gift, it depends on God's generosity, we can prepare through meditation which places us in a position to receive, surrender ourselves to God's love.

However, like Teresa of Avila, Francis also stresses the importance of a virtuous life, as being an essential foundation for contemplation.[46] Francis continually returns to the importance of self-knowledge because not only do we encounter God in prayer but we also encounter the truth about ourselves. There must be a harmony between our life and our prayer or else it is inauthentic. Charity is the gauge of our prayer because it translates our love of God into love of neighbour. Once again Jesus is our model of the virtues, the humble one who shows us the way. It is the lowly virtues of humility, gentleness and simplicity that captivate Francis. These virtues bespeak poverty of spirit, a childlike disposition before God which is essential for entry into the kingdom.

CHAPTER FIVE

Gentle and Humble of Heart

> I love especially these three little virtues: gentleness in the heart, poverty in the spirit and simplicity in life. And also, the rougher exercises: visiting the sick, serving the poor, comforting the afflicted and the like, but everything without impetuosity, but in true freedom.[1]

Francis lived at a time of religious wars and he soon came to realise that the medium is the message. In his debates with those who held contrary viewpoints, he always maintained a respect and courtesy for the other. The truth has its own power and so does not need to be defended with force. This is evident in the early period of his ministerial life when he went to the Chablais region as a missionary. He was received with a certain amount of hostility and, at first, it seemed a fruitless exercise. Since people did not come to church, he decided to go to them and thus began his mission of circulating leaflets and inviting open air debates. These circulars became his first writings, called *The Controversies*.[2] He quickly came to realise that it was impossible to be Christ's disciple without gentleness:

> 'Our Lord, he would add, had founded his doctrine on these words: Be my disciples for I am gentle and humble of heart' (Mt 11:29). Why does God attract us? Because he is kind: 'The Spirit of gentleness, the saint taught, is the Spirit of God.'[3]

Francis emphasises two qualities of love as revealed by Jesus: meekness and humility of heart. Meekness is gentleness towards oneself and one's neighbour and humility is standing in the truth before God, recognising that everything we have, we have received from God and that we depend on him our Creator.

This gentleness requires that we repress the movements of anger, that we are gentle, cordial, and full of meekness towards everybody, that we forgive our enemies, and suffer contempt … 'happy are the gentle, they will possess the earth'; by these words he destroys the pride and arrogance on which the world bases its happiness.[4]

We can see that, for Francis, the teachings of our Lord totally abolish the wisdom of the world and lead us to embrace the folly of the cross. What is this gentleness that is a beatitude (gift) but leads to the cross? Look at the gentleness of Jesus that leads to him being broken on the cross. It would seem from this understanding that gentleness is not the way of 'arrogance and pride' but rather chooses the humble path, the way of lowliness. As such, it would seem to lead us into suffering, where we don't have any power.

Francis, himself, attracted people by his gentleness. St Vincent de Paul described him as the person most like Our Lord because of his gentleness. He had learned from Jesus who is 'meek and humble of heart'. However, this did not come naturally to Francis. Vaugelas heard him say, 'that by nature he was most prone to sudden fits of anger, but that every day he tried to cope with himself'.[5] All his life he had to overcome these temptations. Even in 1619, in Paris, he admitted to a friend: 'I very nearly let go my anger and I was obliged to grip my anger by the scruff of the neck.'[6] He confessed, around this time, that he still 'felt feelings of anger in his heart' and that he had 'to take the reins in both hands to hold it back'.[7]

This was a life-long task for Francis who had to struggle with his own temperament to allow God's grace transform him in the area of gentleness. On occasions his gentleness was not appreciated by the strong-willed Madame de Chantal: 'your gentleness, she said to him, will increase the insolence of these mischievous people.' 'Not at all, not at all, he answered, besides, dear daughter, would you like me to destroy in a quarter of an hour of anger the little edifice of interior peace I have been building up patiently for myself for the last eighteen years?'[8]

There was another incident in 1607 when a commander of Malta barged into his room and insulted Francis because one of his students had failed an exam for a parish benefice (he was more expert at courting women than commenting on the gospel!) He left just as angry and his brother, Jean François, asked him how it was that he had not lost his temper. Francis replied, 'at the time and at many other times he was seething with anger like water in a boiling pot over the fire but that by the grace of God, even if the violent efforts to resist such passion endangered his life … he would not let himself go'.[9]

GENTLENESS TOWARDS ONESELF AS

AN EXPRESSION OF LOVING ONESELF

As a spiritual director, Francis realised that if you want to be gentle towards others, then you need to begin by being gentle with yourself.

> One of the best exercises for gentleness is to be patient with ourselves and our imperfections.[10]

Some personalities find this more difficult than others, because although they are very demanding and critical of others, they are even more so of themselves, and they never reach the level of perfection they set themselves. Francis recognises this in those he directs and he counsels them:

> Our heart needs to be corrected, gently and calmly, and not to be vexed more and troubled. We ought to say to it: 'Well now, my heart, my friend, in the name of God take courage; let us go on, let us beware of ourselves, let us lift ourselves up to our help and our God.'[11]

If we are gentle with ourselves and accepting of ourselves then, this will effect our relationship with others. Often the problem is not the other, but really ourselves. If there are areas within ourselves that we do not look upon with compassion, that we would like to be different, that we exclude, would wish not to be there, that we relegate to the margins – then what we do with ourselves we do with others. If we do not love the prodigal part of ourselves, then our attitude will be that of the older son.

Once we get in touch with our heart, we are less 'insecure', we don't see others who disagree with us as a threat, someone to be changed so that they see things the same way as I do. It is when I operate out of my wounded sensibility that I forsake gentleness, and the other certainly doesn't experience me as being gentle! Gentleness makes hospitality possible. This is why Francis warns against opening the door to anger under any pretext, because 'there never was an angry man who thought his anger unjust'.[12] What Francis recommends is in harmony with the scriptural advice not to let the sun go down on your anger. It is better to correct an angry word or deed with 'an act of meekness toward the person you were angry with'.[13] Quoting St Augustine he writes:

It is better to deny entrance to just and reasonable anger than to admit it, no matter how small it is. Once let in, it is driven out again only with difficulty. It comes in as a little twig and in less than no time it grows big and becomes a beam. If anger can only gain the night on us and if the sun sets on it, which the apostle forbids, it turns into hatred, from which we have hardly any way of ridding ourselves.[14]

Unresolved anger opens the door to resentment which leads to a hardening of heart, making gentleness virtually impossible. The remedy to anger, it would appear, is to repair it 'instantly by a contrary act of meekness. Fresh wounds are quickest healed, as the saying goes.'[15]

Our lack of gentleness towards others is often rooted in our lack of gentleness towards ourselves.[16] Even when we speak of conversion, this must be done by love and gentleness. This does not mean that we cannot be challenged. Francis recognises that in order to grow we need to leave behind certain patterns of behaviour that imprison us in selfishness. But this very struggle to overcome our self and grow in love, must be done with gentleness. Growth needs to be assisted by our efforts, but we cannot force growth. We prepare the ground to allow growth to take place. In this respect, Francis' teaching is in harmony with the parable of the darnel and the wheat (Mt 13:24-30). We are not to pull up the weeds for fear that we might also uproot the wheat. Furthermore, what we regard as 'weeds' may turn out to be our wheat and vice-versa. Gentleness with ourselves ensures that the process of growth continues in its proper season.

This is the essence of Salesian spirituality, that love is the means and the end of perfection: love must be the principal even of conversion. By doing this, he transfigures ascesis: we could speak of an ascesis of love in his spirituality. It is necessary to struggle against self-love but it must be done through love. St Francis begins reform by the interior and not the exterior.

As we are fallen, wounded, we have to work at restoring our image in Christ, co-operating with God's grace. However, this work must be done by gentleness, because gentleness is the principle that allows for growth, and growth cannot be forced. It can be encouraged, the ground can be prepared, it can be nourished but it cannot be forced. Love is gentle and kind; this allows for compassion towards oneself and one's neighbour. This is why Francis insists in a proper attitude towards one's own body, not to pamper it, but to reverence it:

> I have always judged that it was a spirit of profound humility towards God, and of great sweetness towards our neighbour; so that having less bodily austerity, there must be more sweetness of heart … Humility towards God, then, and gentleness towards our neighbour, must in your houses supply the place of the austerity of others.[17]

Why does love need gentleness? Because love by its essence is full of zeal, it is impatient, it cannot bear delays, it is a passion of the heart, it impels the desire towards its object and becomes irritated or worried by delays or obstacles; but it is gentleness that calms its impatience. Gentleness renders love patient. Therefore, in a trial gentle love is strong whereas an impetuous love would not be. This leads us to acknowledge one of Francis' best known maxims: there is nothing as strong as gentleness and nothing as gentle as real strength.

HUMILITY OF HEART

> True humility does not make a show of itself and hardly
> speaks in a humble way. It not only wants to conceal all other
> virtues but most of all it wants to conceal itself.[18]

In each of us there is to be found perfection and imperfection.
Humility which is the least, but most necessary, of all the virtues
is nothing else than a recognition of this aspect of ourselves, a
sign that we are creatures and not the Creator, that we are imperfect.

> I do not say an awareness but rather a recognition of this be-
> cause there are plenty who know they are nothing but don't
> want to recognise it! … Humility is not to take away from
> our greatness but rather is a just and proper evaluation of
> who we are, i.e. the greatness of God in us.[19]

It would appear that Francis is keen to avoid two extremes: an
unrealistic, over-inflated sense of self, and one derived from a
poor self image which leads to the abasement of self:

> Know thyself must be understood not only of the knowledge
> of our misery and vileness, but also of that of the excellence
> and dignity of our souls, which are capable of being united to
> the Divinity by his divine goodness … Humility makes us
> distrust ourselves, and generosity makes us trust in God –
> they never are and never can be separated, it is a false and
> foolish humility which prevents people from looking at the
> good that God has placed in them.[20]

This is where Francis warns of a false sense of humility, which is
interior, that is where people are unwilling to acknowledge the
gifts and graces that they have been given:

> Many people neither wish nor dare to think over and reflect
> on the particular graces God has shown them because they
> are afraid that this might arouse vainglory and self-complac-
> ence. They deceive themselves in this, since the true means to
> attain the love of God is consideration of his benefits.[21]

And he continues:

> Let us consider what he has done for us and what we have
> done against him, and as we reflect on our sins one by one let

us also consider his graces one by one. There is no need to fear that knowledge of his gifts will make us proud if only we remember this truth, that none of the good in us comes from ourselves.[22]

First of all, note that humility is linked to truth, back to our original understanding that we are imperfect but made by God who is good; therefore, the goodness in us is because of God. Once we lose sight of this we lose sight of the truth of our being and fall into a pseudo-humility which is unable to recognise things as gift. There is no need to fear the truth. If something is there which is good, then we need to recognise it as gift. Note the tremendous balance present in his writing. He will not allow us simply to dwell on our sinfulness, because it is not the whole story. We can only do so, if we also take into consideration the love of God, or the God who loves us in our sinfulness. Without this, we would deprive ourselves of hope which would lead us to despair. Francis goes further:

> The humble person is all the more courageous because he recognises his own impotence. The more wretched he esteems himself the more daring he becomes because he places his whole trust in God who rejoices to display his power in our weakness and raise up his mercy on our misery.[23]

It is here that we have the essence of Christian humility, that our weakness and imperfection becomes the place where God can bestow his goodness and mercy. Indeed, Francis writes:

> Among beggars, those who are the most miserable and whose sores are the largest and most loathsome think themselves the best beggars and the most likely to draw alms. We are but beggars; the most miserable are the best off. The mercy of God willingly looks on them.[24]

The acknowledgement of our weakness and imperfection does not deprive us of hope. On the contrary, this realistic awareness of the shadow side of ourselves turns us towards the goodness of God with great confidence:

> Humility consists not only in distrusting ourselves, but also

in trusting in God; and the distrust of ourselves and of our own strength produces confidence in God; and from this confidence springs the generosity of spirit of which we are speaking.[25]

PRACTICAL CONSIDERATIONS IN RELATION TO HUMILITY

1. Consistent with his thought in general, like his advice on mortification and asceticism, Francis states that the best form of humility is the humility you do not choose, but comes your way.

If you wish to know what are the best kinds of abjection, Philothea, I tell you plainly that the ones most profitable to our souls and most acceptable to God are those which come to us accidentally or because of our state in life. The reason is that we have not chosen them ourselves but have accepted them as sent by God and his choice is always better than our own.[26]

Francis goes to some length to point out that we cannot compare 'our' humility with that of another:

It may be that a sister whom you see fall very often, and commit many imperfections, may be more virtuous and more pleasing to God, either by the great courage she keeps up amidst her imperfections, not letting herself be troubled or disturbed at seeing herself so liable to fall, or by the humility she derives from it, or again by the love of her abjection, than another, who may have a dozen virtues, natural or acquired, and has less exercise and trial and perhaps in consequence less courage and humility, than the other whom you see so subject to failures.

2. Francis often says that when we find ourselves attacked by a particular vice, then we must practice the contrary virtue. A practical way of showing humility towards others is, as soon as 'you see that you are guilty of an angry deed, correct the fault right away by an act of meekness toward the person you were angry with.'[27]

3. Sometimes our anger can be directed at ourselves, when we

realise that we are not as perfect as we thought or would like. We must not fret over our own imperfections. These fits of anger and vexation against ourselves tend to pride and they spring from no other source than self-love, which is disturbed and upset at seeing that it is imperfect. Thus, we also need to exercise meekness towards ourselves:

> Lift up your heart again whenever it falls, but do so meekly by humbling yourself before God through knowledge of your own misery and do not be surprised if you fall. It is no wonder that infirmity should be infirm, weakness weak, or misery wretched. Nevertheless, detest with all your powers the offence God has received from you and with great courage and confidence in his mercy return to the path of virtue you had forsaken.[28]

What we have to avoid is a pseudo-humility which is really a form of self-pity, when we fail we recognise our weakness and declare that I am fit for nothing – and then we pass into discouragement which makes us say there is no hope for me![29]

4. There is no other way of acquiring this, or any other virtue, than by repeated acts.[30] These acts come from an inner disposition; exterior humility is dependent on an inner humility. Yet, these exterior expressions are important because, as Francis says, humble services and matters of exterior humility are only the rind, but this preserves the fruit.

> Some men become proud and overbearing because they ride a fine horse, wear a feather in their hat, or are dressed in a splendid suit of clothes … If there is any glory in such things it belongs to the horse, the bird and the tailor.[31]

Humility: A descending charity

Francis describes humility as a 'descending charity' – this descending (movement) of love is exemplified in the person of Jesus when he unites himself to our nature in the incarnation. He describes the descending movement as follows:

> He poured himself completely into us and, so to speak, dis-

solved his grandeur so as to reduce it to the form and figure of our littleness. Because of this he is called the fountain of living water, dew or rain come down from heaven.[32]

This variation of the Pauline Hymn (Phil 2:7) attests to the downward movement, the kenosis of Jesus, but also reminds us that he humbles himself so that he can exalt us, raise us up to the dignity of the children of God.[33] Thus, there is also an ascending movement:

He divested himself of his grandeur, his glory ... he annihilated himself to fill us with his divinity, to fulfill us with his goodness, to raise us up to his dignity and give us the divine being of children of God.[34]

Meekness and humility of heart reveal a heart of love; they are indispensable qualities of love. It is this humility and gentleness that points to the sacrificial aspect of love, because love goes out of itself towards the other. This aspect of love is called ecstasy by Francis de Sales. There is a tremendous consistency with Francis in this regard because creation, the incarnation, and redemption are all the fruit of this ecstatic love. Through creation we are made in the image of God and through the incarnation God is made in our image. Thus, we are called to enter into this movement of love by becoming one in Christ. Looking at the person of Jesus we can see this downward movement (humility and gentleness) first by becoming a child and entering into our flesh, and then by going even further and sacrificing his humanity on the cross. And yet, it is not only the incarnation and crucifixion that reveals this logic of the downward movement of God in Christ to raise us up, but his whole life and preaching. The washing of the disciples' feet (Jn 13) exemplifies this. See the humility of Christ who divests himself, wraps a towel around him and begins to wash the feet of his disciples. Note the position: he leaves the table, moves downwards, and takes their feet to wash them (explaining the meaning of Eucharist, same movement). The disciples are looking down on him, he is looking up at them. The position is symbolic in the sense that not only does it signify God's movement downwards to become one with us, but it also makes it real, makes it present. So what do we learn from him who is 'meek and humble of heart' in this situation?

We learn that humility is not so much a question of feeling little (this could be an inferiority complex rather than true humility) nor is it a question of even being little (because it is possible to be little and not humble) but rather of choosing to 'make ourselves little'. Perfect humility consists, therefore, in constantly making oneself small, not for the sake of some personal need or benefit, but for the sake of love – to elevate others.[35]

That's what the humility of Jesus was like; he made himself so small as to annihilate himself for us. What Francis, quoting Paul, says of the poverty of Jesus also throws light on his humility:

Though he was rich, for your sake he became poor, so that by his poverty you might become rich (2 Cor 8:9).

He divested himself of his grandeur, his glory … he annihilated himself to fill us with his divinity, to fulfill us with his good-ness, to raise us up to his dignity and give us the divine being of children of God.

As we can see, the humility Jesus reveals to us is a lowering of himself, not so much in thought, word or sentiment as in deed. Now we know what Jesus means when he says 'learn from me for I am humble of heart'. It is an invitation to make ourselves small for love, to wash, as he did, our neighbour's feet. This new side of humility can be summarised in the word *service:*

If any one would be first, he must be last of all and servant of all. (Mk 9:35)

Even as the Son of Man came not to be served, but to serve. (Mt 20:28)

Thus, humility helps us to enter into the movement of love, a lowering of oneself. In the words of Francis, humility is 'a de-scending charity' where love becomes service. Love is active.

Love, then, is not about going up the ladder of success; it is about the movement down the ladder into weakness. It's the washing of the feet, the lowering of oneself, going out of oneself

for the good of the other. It is the path of littleness, not of great-
ness, the little virtues, not unlike the 'little way' of St Thérèse of
Lisieux.[36] It is this movement, this emptying that creates the
space within us so that we can receive love and become love.

It naturally follows from the above considerations that
gentleness and humility lead to the virtue of simplicity. At the
heart of simplicity is a childlike trust and confidence in God.
Since this virtue is of paramount importance in the spirituality
of St Francis de Sales, we will devote the next chapter to it. This
disposition of simplicity towards God is an essential require-
ment for entry into the kingdom of God.

CHAPTER SIX

Childlike Simplicity

Unless you become like a little child, you will not enter into the kingdom of heaven. (Mt 18:3)

Consistently in the gospels we have this pronouncement of Jesus, that only the childlike will inherit the kingdom of God. The kingdom of God is to be received and, therefore, demands the openness of a child. A child allows the father or mother to give gifts. It is this childlike quality that is the hallmark of Salesian spirituality. Simplicity understood in terms of a child who is open to receive:

> Certainly, children, whom our Lord tells us should be our model of perfection, are, generally speaking, quite free from care, especially in the presence of their fathers and mothers. They cling to them, without turning to consider their satisfaction or their consolations. These they presume in good faith, and enjoy in simplicity, without any curiosity whatsoever as to their causes or effects. Love occupies them sufficiently without their doing anything else.[1]

A child has a form of love that we often lose as adults. This love is to trust instinctively. It is to place oneself in the hands of another with complete trust. A child is dependent, relies on the other. Marked by life's experiences in which trust has been broken, we end up defending ourselves. As adults, we can replace trust with control and self-sufficiency. This, in turn, effects our relationships with others, God and ourselves.

Francis calls us back to the 'maturity of the child'. This is the paradox of the gospel. It is the child who is held up as the model of the spiritual life. The spiritual journey involves a certain homecoming where we become a child again who instinctively trusts in God:

> A child, when very young, is in a state of such simplicity that he has no knowledge of anything but of his mother. He has only one love, which is for his mother, and in that love only one aim and desire – his mother's breast. When he is upon that beloved breast, he wants nothing more. The soul that has attained perfect simplicity has only one love, which is for God. In this love it has only one aim, to rest upon the bosom of the heavenly Father, and there to abide like a beloved child, leaving all care of itself to that good Father. This soul is anxious about nothing except to maintain this holy confidence.[2]

This childlike trust is a process. We do not trust once and for all, but each little act of trust increases our capacity to trust more. This will vary with each person because of one's personal history. For some people it is easy to trust instinctively, for others it will be much more difficult. Grace builds on nature. However, Francis is adamant that a lot of our difficulties in life arise whenever we lose this childlike focus on God. When we lose this single-mindedness of purpose many distractions get in the way and our energies are dispersed. He alludes to the Martha and Mary text to illustrate this point:

> Do you not see that although Martha's desire to show great hospitality to Our Lord was laudable, yet she was reproved by the divine Master because she added another motive to the good object that made her so eager to serve him? So, to the first pure aim of the love of God, she added many little secondary motives, for which she was reproved by Our Lord.[3]

In this respect we can be our own worst enemy when we lose this single-mindedness and get worried over many things. Francis continues that being worried about what others think of us can take up our time and energy, and again we have lost our single-mindedness. Another obstacle to simplicity is wherever we get preoccupied with our spiritual advancement, wondering if we are prospering on our spiritual journey. Whilst Francis acknowledges the importance of self-knowledge, he also warns of the dangers of preoccupation with the self that can lead to introspection. We need to achieve a balance between growing in self-awareness and preoccupation with self, 'as human nature can never stop short at the golden mean, but generally speaking, runs to extremes'.[4]

Once again we are to model ourselves on the child who is not preoccupied with self, but abandons itself to the parent with trust and simplicity. It follows that if we come to appreciate ourselves as children of God, then, this reveals not only who we are in relation to God, but also who God is in relation to us. Francis' writing is imbued with images that attest to the Fatherly-Motherly love of God for us.

A FATHERLY-MOTHERLY LOVE

Probably the most striking images that express the love of God in the *Treatise* are those which evoke the fatherly-motherly tenderness of God. Francis moves naturally from male to female images in an attempt to capture the wholeness of God's love which is like that of a father and that of a mother:

> Our Lord ... is like a good father or a good mother who allows his child to walk alone when he is in a meadow or large field because if he falls, he will not come to much harm; but in dangerous and rugged paths, he is carried carefully in his arms.[5]

This image of being 'carried' expresses both the concern of a father and a mother for their child and hence is used frequently by Francis.[6] At one point he states, 'O God, Father eternal, what is there that your children, chicks that live under your wings, have to fear?'[7] However, earlier he has used the same image to describe the maternal quality of God's love, like that of a jealous mother hen protecting her chicks:

> The hen is merely a hen, that is an animal without any courage or spirit whatsoever, as long as she is not yet a mother.

> But when she becomes a mother, she takes on a lion's heart, always holds her head up, always keeps her eyes on watch, always darts glances on every side for no matter how small a sign of danger to her little ones. There is no enemy at whose eyes she will not fly in defence of her dear brood, for which she has constant care that causes her to go about constantly clucking and complaining.[8]

It is interesting to note the phrases that embody this maternal love which reveals an almost 'masculine' strength. For example, it is a love which has a 'lion's heart', 'defends', and is 'constant'.[9]

The question at issue is not one of gender because God is beyond male and female sexuality. However, it is by combining both the male and female experience that Francis attempts to reveal something which is analogous to the infinite love of God. It is the totality of a mother's and father's love that best approximates the superabundance of God's parental love. Hence, as we have already stated, Francis moves without difficulty from masculine to feminine images to evoke this reality. The following citation is a good example of this juxtaposition of female and male imagery:

> A mother is not satisfied with feeding her babe with her milk, which is her own substance, unless she herself gives her own flowerlike breasts to her child's mouth. This is so that it may not merely receive its mother's substance from a spoon or some other utensil, but from her own substance and in her own substance. Thus the mother's own substance serves both as vessel and as nourishment received by her beloved child. In like manner, God our Father is not content to make us receive his own substance into our mind, that is to make us see his divinity. Out of the depths of his mercy he himself applies his substance to our minds, so that we no longer understand him by means of a representation or image but in his very substance and by his very substance.[10]

In such a portrayal we are not dealing with a dualistic representation of God in which female imagery is used to soften a rather strict, paternal figure. On the contrary, the female and male images describe a single reality, that of the tender love of God. However, this tenderness can best be imaged by appealing to the diverse experiences of fatherhood and motherhood which help to give different shades to the portrait of God's love. What is common to both is that they embody the tender love of God.

Concretely, this tenderness of God's love is manifested in the manner in which he does not give us a 'representation', but rather his very 'substance' just as a mother feeds her child with 'her own substance'. This maternal-paternal 'nourishing' finds its supreme expression in the eucharistic Jesus who nourishes us with his body, 'the perpetual feast of divine grace'.[11]

It seems apparent, then, that by having recourse to maternal-paternal imagery, Francis is keen to emphasise the relational nature of God. Not only is God in relation to us, but God is in an intimate relationship with us which can best be imaged by the bond that exists between father-mother and child. It is his intention to arouse the reader to respond to the love of God:

Who could not love his royal heart, so fatherly maternal towards us?[12]

This is the God who we are being asked to trust. This is central to Salesian spirituality, because it is the caring face of God as revealed by Jesus – the God of Jesus. The Salesian view begins with the love of God and, therefore, he prefers to use images not representative of power like King, Lord etc., but rather, as we have seen, images of the caring parent, be it mother or father.[13] An Henri Lemaire writes:

It seems that the image of the child in its mother's or father's arms holds central place, where previous to him it was the image of the judge or the Master with his servant or slave.[14]

Having demonstrated the Salesian use of female and male imagery to convey the tender love of God, it is now our intention to proceed to examine them separately in order to discover the nuances that they bring to a portrayal of God's love.

A FATHERLY LOVE

Francis, like St Teresa of Avila, is fascinated by the fact that through friendship with Jesus we share in his intimacy with the Father. We can say with him, 'Our Father':

> Thus should ye pray: Our Father. He is called 'Father', not Lord or ruler or Judge. The name of Father is Christ's normal description of God.[15]

The conception of God as Father bespeaks a complex reality which includes, at one and the same time, tenderness and reverence. Francis borrows language from the courtly tradition[16] to express the majesty, sovereignty of God as Father:

> When a Prince walks among blind men, they do not see him so they do not honour him. When told about him they acknowledge him, but soon forget him, because they do not see him. Unfortunately, we do not see God, so we often forget he is there, or hold back on the honour due to him … prostrate yourself before his divine majesty. Acknowledge that you are unworthy to appear before such sovereign majesty.[17]

This idea of the legal relationship and idea of God as King, prevalent in the Ignatian system of thought, is also present in the Salesian imaging of God.[18] However, whereas for Ignatius it is contemplating on the divine majesty of God that will awaken love, Francis from the first moment considers love to be the central point. In his use of the kingly image, it is less a question of authority than love:

> The gentle King marries the soul which becomes his beloved son or daughter, no longer his servant or slave; the heavenly King yields himself to our recreation.[19]

This love is made supremely visible in the kenotic act of the King's Son who dies for us, revealing the infinite condescension of the divine Monarch, 'resigning his throne of incomprehensible majesty'.[20]

The sovereign majesty of God provokes a certain 'fear' which comes from 'the natural knowledge which God has providen-

tially given to us, and makes us recognise how completely we
are dependent on his all-sovereign power by arousing us to im-
plore his help.'[21] Francis is careful to distinguish this type of fear
from our normal understanding of fear. Here is intended the
biblical notion of fear in the sense of filial respect:

> Therefore those men fear God with filial affection who fear to
> displease him purely and simply because he is their sweet,
> most benign, and most loving Father.[22]

Such filial fear does not exclude the idea of an all-loving, tender
Father, as imaged in the return of the prodigal son:

> Thus, in addition to the thousand caresses that the prodigal
> son received from his father, he was established anew and in
> an even better way in all his privileges and in all the graces,
> favours, and dignities he had lost.[23]

The motive for such lavishing of affection on a wayward son, is
quite simply the prodigal love of the father who 'although the
prodigal son returned naked, filthy, stinking, his fond father
takes him into his arms, kisses him lovingly, weeps on his shoulder because he is his Father and a Father's heart feels for his
child'.[24] It is this biblical notion of fatherhood, of the tender love
of Abba-Father that dominates the writings of St Francis:

> God who calls us to himself is watching to see how we are
> faring and will never allow anything to happen to us which
> is not for our greater good. He knows who we are, and will
> hold out his fatherly hand to us when we stumble, so that
> nothing may stop us … He has watched over you till now; all
> you have to do is keep a tight hold on the hand of Providence
> and God will help you in all that happens, and where you
> cannot walk he will carry you in his arms. What need you
> fear, my very dear daughter, since you belong to God who
> has told us so firmly that 'to them that love God all things
> work together unto good'? … What can a child fear in the
> arms of such a father? Really try to be a little child, my very
> dear daughter; and as you know, children don't have a lot of
> things to worry about because they have others to think for
> them; they are really strong if they stay close to their father.

So do this, my very dear daughter, and you will have peace.[25]

Throughout the *Treatise* God is imaged as a tender, loving Father who desires that we clasp his hand in filial abandonment so that he can lead us to happiness.[26] In book nine, chapter fourteen of the *Treatise*, he distinguishes between two ways of conforming to the will of God: The first is to allow ourselves to be led by God our heavenly Father by holding his hand; The second and more perfect way of abandonment is to allow ourselves to be 'carried by his divine good pleasure, just as a little child is carried in its mother's arms.'[27] This juxtaposition of paternal and maternal love leads us naturally to examine in detail how Francis images divine tenderness through the use of female imagery.

A MOTHERLY LOVE

The image of mother and child to express the tender love of God is one that pervades the *Treatise*.[28] By imaging God in this way, Francis is well within the biblical tradition.[29] It is also to be found in many monastic writings, for example, Bernard of Clairvaux, Anselm of Canterbury, Meister Eckhart, Julian of Norwich and, of course, Teresa of Avila. The biblical and Catholic traditions provide a rich heritage for Francis to draw upon, but one can't help but think that his own life experience is an important source for this image. Being the eldest of a large family, Francis must have constantly witnessed his mother with a baby at the breast or a toddler at her knee.[30] It is from reflecting on this human experience that Francis concludes that a mother's love embodies the deepest form of unconditional and active love:

> Maternal love is the most urgent, the most active, and the most ardent of all forms of love, since it is an indefatigable and insatiable love.[31]

In describing this paragon of love, we should note the adjectives he uses: 'active', 'ardent', 'indefatigable' and 'insatiable'. If these are characteristics of a mother's love, then how much more are they expressive of the divine love.

It is with the eye of an artist that Francis observes the relationship between mother and child as being indicative of God's
tender love for us:

> Consider, then, a beautiful little child to whom the seated
> mother offers her breast. It throws itself forcibly into her
> arms and gathers up and entwines all its little body on that
> beloved bosom and breast. See how its mother in turn takes it
> in, clasps it, fastens it so to speak to her bosom, joins her
> mouth to its mouth, and kisses it. Watch again how that little
> babe is allured by its mother's caresses, and how on its part it
> co-operates in this union of its mother and itself. As much as
> it possibly can, it fastens and presses itself to its mother's
> breast and face. It seems as if it wants to bury and hide itself
> completely in the beloved bosom from which it came.
> Theotimus, at such a moment there is a perfect union; it is but
> a single union, yet it proceeds from both mother and child al-
> though in such wise that it depends entirely on the mother.
> She drew the child to herself. She first clasped it in her arms
> and pressed it to her bosom. The child's strength was never
> sufficient to clasp and hold itself so close to its mother.[32]

An analysis of this quotation reveals the 'active' nature of a
mother's love and, consequently, God's love. It is a love which
'offers', 'clasps and fastens' us to his bosom, and 'kisses' us.
Once again the image reveals a theological reality that God's
love, which is without measure, always precedes our response.
It is the mother who actively leads, nourishes and holds her
child. It is the supreme image of selfless love and complete self-
giving. It is an image which serves to vividly capture the reality
of God's 'need' to give and our need to receive:

> The suckling child is urged on by its need, while the mother
> who gives him her milk is urged on by her own abundance.[33]

A mother quite simply rejoices in the fact that her child is content. Henri Lemaire, in speaking of Francis's use of maternal imagery, states that 'the image teaches us, but above all it wants to
arouse us, to seduce our whole being'.[34] After the evocation of
the maternal attentiveness of God we are asked to have a firm

trust in that gentleness:

> Therefore a hundred times during the day we should turn our gaze upon God's loving will, make our will melt into it, and devoutly cry out, 'O God of infinite sweetness, how amiable is your will and how desirable are your favours! You have created us for eternal life, and your maternal bosom, with its sacred breasts swelling with incomparable love, abounds in the milk of mercy, whether to pardon penitents or to make perfect the just. Ah, why do we not fasten our wills to yours, like children who attach themselves to their mothers' breasts, to draw out the milk of your eternal blessings!'[35]

The image of being carried by the mother seeks, above all, to arouse us to filial abandonment. Emphasis is placed on our need for a childlike disposition[36] to receive that which God seeks to give:

> We simply let ourselves be carried by his divine good pleasure, just as a little child is carried in its mother's arms, by a certain kind of admirable consent which may be called the union, or rather the unity of our will with that of God. This is the way in which we should strive to let ourselves be borne forward in the will of God's good pleasure. The effects of this will of good pleasure proceed purely from his providence.[37]

This image of the child resting in its mother's arms expresses a fundamental theme in the works of St Francis de Sales, that of loving conformity to God's will.[38] It is an image familiar to us, but we must not forget that in Francis's epoch the most predominant images to express our relationship with God were those of the Judge or Master with his servant. This difference is significant.[39] Perhaps it is the most revolutionary aspect of the *Treatise*, as Buckley points out:

> Perhaps the most startling development in the *Treatise* has passed unnoticed. It lies with his understanding of God. The divine Majesty has given way to a God who is profoundly maternal.[40]

It is this use of maternal imagery that best conveys the tenderness of an all-loving God and therefore, adds a certain distinctiveness to the Salesian vision of God's love. If God is mother for Francis, then it is impossible for him to think of God as a distant or forbidding judge who seeks to condemn or destroy the creation which he has made.

Why are these images so central? Because it is through these images that Francis teaches us and encourages us to trust God and let God carry us without worry, but in total abandonment. The images lead us to a doctrine of confidence and peace.[41] Through these very images of mother-father and child, Francis encourages us to reflect on our own behaviour as regards God.

CHAPTER 7

Trust and Confidence in God

When Francis speaks about confidence to the Visitation Sisters, in nearly every spiritual conference, he bases his counsels on the certainty of the love of God for us:

> You wish further to know the foundation our confidence ought to have? It must be grounded on the infinite goodness of God and on the merits of the death and passion of Our Lord Jesus Christ, with this condition on our part, that we should preserve and recognise in ourselves an entire and firm resolution to belong wholly to God and to abandon ourselves in all things and without any reserve to his providence.[1]

It is not ourselves that we are trusting but the goodness of God. We trust God not because we are good, but because God is good. God continues to be faithful to us, even when we are unfaithful to him.[2] Francis then is trying to reveal to us what is revealed in Jesus – that God is love. Love is the beginning, middle and end for Francis. Which is why we should have confidence in God – because he loves us. Thus, the images employed by Francis are an attempt to evoke a response in us that will encourage us to respond with confidence and trust in God:

> 'Our friend God…' The love of the friend absolutely transcends the good that one can expect from him.[3]

It is of utmost importance that this is established, because when we are led along the road of surrender and abandonment, trust and confidence are essential. Why? Because naturally we are moving from security to insecurity, we are moving from being in control to allowing ourselves be led. The natural response is

one of fear, anxiety and resistance. Why? Because if we let go
where will we end up? Francis repeats that we are allowing ourselves to surrender into the hands of a God who loves us, a God
who keeps his promises. Let's not get romantic notions about
this. It is not easy to surrender. We will most probably not have
any feelings of consolation. But it is not about feelings ultimately,
it is the path of faith, of trust.

PROVIDENCE

Abandon is only made possible by a belief in providence.
Francis goes to great lengths to repeat this continually to the
Visitation Sisters. Providence is trusting that God will provide,
trusting that God is interested, trusting that God is active. It is
only when we know intimately that God is seeking to establish a
personal relationship with us that our trust can truly flourish
and blossom:

> It is very true that we must have great confidence in order
> thus to abandon ourselves, without reserve, to Divine
> Providence; but also, when we abandon everything, our
> Lord takes care of everything and arranges everything.[4]

And Francis says yet again:

> Our Lord leads us by the hand and does with us works for
> which he asks our co-operation. Go therefore ... to the work
> for which God has chosen you. He will be at your right hand,
> so that no difficulty will shake you. He will hold you with his
> hand so that you may follow his way. He has watched over
> you till now; all you have to do is keep a tight hold on the
> hand of providence and God will help you in all that hap-
> pens, and where you cannot walk he will carry you in his
> arms. What need you fear since you belong to God who has
> told us so firmly that to them that love God all things work
> together unto good?[5]

Francis continually recommends the sisters to unite their will to
God's providence, in particular in difficult circumstances where
we don't understand the why, where we don't have any answers

to the questions we ask – why does it have to happen like this?

It is then we need to trust in the providence of God, have confidence in God. Because while we are here on earth the human spirit often gets 'twisted in the threads of a thousand difficulties'.[6] It demands a great level of trust and faith to comply with Francis' advice to a woman who is suffering great physical pain. He writes:

> I cannot ask him to do anything for you except that he would fashion your heart in total accordance with his will, in order to lodge and reign therein eternally ... Whether he does it with the hammer, or with the chisel, or with the brush, it is for him to act according to his pleasure.[7]

But once again to restore our confidence in God despite the painful situation we may find ourselves in, Francis reminds us that God may permit obstacles to purify our hope, but he is also the same Father who lifts his child in the face of obstacles.[8] Francis doesn't allow us to reduce God's ways to our own. We cannot control God. And yet, for the person who loves God, all things work out for good.

If we examine closely the images of Francis in relation to spiritual abandonment, in particular the child-parent ones, we notice this immediately. Henri Lemaire points out that it is not the passivity of Quietists.[9] God asks us to take 'our small steps' and 'to hold his hand':

> This soul which has abandoned itself has nothing else to do but to *remain* in the arms of Our Lord, like a child on the breast of its mother; which, when she puts it down to walk, walks till she takes it up again, and when she chooses to carry it, lets her do so: it does not know nor think where it is going, *but lets itself be carried or led* where its mother pleases.[10]

It is true that before God one must assume an attitude of surrender which demands a certain passivity.[11] However, for this to happen we need to take small steps to ensure that we are receptive to God's grace. It is an active passivity, if you like. We need to do all we can to create an openness to receive from God. But how do we manage to do this? We're back to 'small steps' and 'holding God's hand'. He reiterates: 'all you have to do is to keep a tight hold on the hand of providence and God will help you'; 'Our Lord leads us by the hand and does with us works for which he asks our co-operation'; 'all that is required of you is to place your confidence in him'; 'above all take care not to leave his hand'; 'do like little children who with one of their hands holds on to their father and with the other pick strawberries or blackberries…'[12]

Having cited such a long series of images on abandon, to prevent us from falling into the illusion that Francis recommends a Quietistic passivity it might be useful to recall some of his demands. He repeats that it is necessary to serve both God and neighbour. For 'in the world we can only love God by doing good, therefore, our love must be active'.

The truth of genuine abandonment is seen in how we respond to our neighbour. It is through service to our neighbour that God concretely asks us to choose the way of abandon:

In his mind, great occasions for exhibiting one's devotion rarely presented themselves, but little occasions were there everyday: checking anger, selfishness, and pride in unexpected and ordinary encounters was a good deal more humbling than waiting for a dramatic episode through which one might display one's fervour. In fact, the constant and ordinary repetition of small loving acts was, in his view, the most efficacious means of humility which, in its turn, was the living out of the Jesus of Matthew's gospel.[13]

ABANDON AND LOVE

Francis cannot understand this way of abandon without it being motivated by love. We freely choose to surrender to God and to our neighbour out of love for God. Francis cautions us:

Love is essential to Christian life, but without humility love is impossible, for love is submission and gift of self to the loved ones. Pride does not submit, does not give self: humility alone submits and gives self. Love is kind, it is made of benevolence and compassion; love is gentle, a love which offends is no longer love.[14]

We have already noted that love needs two helpers, humility and gentleness. Yet, it is love which fires the heart to surrender. To whom are we surrendering? We surrender to love.[15]

Surrender, understood as an act of love, brings us face to face with what seems a contradiction. On the one hand, we do nothing, we allow God to work within us, but on the other hand, we have to do something to allow God to work within us. It's the paradox of the gospel. All is gift, God's grace and yet we have to be open to receiving this grace. It's the mystery of the relationship between God's grace and our freedom.

Surrender is a fruit of our trust in God. Surrender, abandon, is an act of trust, a special form of love which is the gift of self into the arms of another. This way of surrender in love expresses one of the fundamental tenets of spirituality – giving oneself over to the discipline of transformation. This is embodied in the Salesian maxim 'ask for nothing, refuse nothing', which we will now explore.

ASK FOR NOTHING, REFUSE NOTHING

Initially the statement 'ask for nothing, refuse nothing' seems a very disturbing statement that appears illogical and impractical. Indeed, it almost appears childish and would seem to be encouraging immaturity. It certainly appears not to be an adult way of responding.

However, once we begin to tease it out, we realise that it does require a childlike attitude of trust. It is a way of following God or allowing oneself to be led by God. It's a recognition that God is not only above us, but ahead of us, before us. It is a way in which we leave God free to lead us and a way which prevents us from trying to manipulate God. Sometimes we can delude ourselves into believing that we are following God, when in fact it is our own construction of God, subtly following self and one's own desires.

This freedom is not only to allow ourselves to be drawn by God, but that we may also reach a place of true freedom within ourselves. Often we are a bundle of conflicting desires. Once we satisfy our surface desires we can often be left feeling frustrated and dissatisfied. Sometimes we can end up being less free and enslaved by these very desires. It is our deeper desires that bring us to a place of greater freedom. Thus, living this maxim would seem, at first, to lessen our freedom. However, it is designed in such a way that by refusing to ask and allowing God to provide we are led to a place of greater freedom. Genuine spirituality recognises a close link between our deepest desires and the will of God. This is to be expected when we accept that the 'love of God has been poured into our hearts by the Holy Spirit which has been given us' (Rom 5:5).

Our way of operating may often be a way of being in control and trying to bring things about in our way, in our time. The maxim 'ask for nothing, refuse nothing' challenges us to operate with a totally different rhythm. This maxim makes great demands of us, because it challenges us to let go of control and to trust God. It is encouraging us to get beyond the control of our ego. It is not offering us self-fulfillment, but self-transcendence.

It requires a contemplative stance, it demands patience and receptivity. We are to allow things to happen in God's time and in God's way. It is an active passivity that is required of us – certainly we must wait, but we must be watchful and prepared:

Do not, however, confuse patience with indifference, laziness or lack of common sense. When you are overtaken by misfortune, seek whatever remedies God affords you. Not to do so would be tempting his divine providence. When, however, you have done whatever you can do, used whatever God has put within your reach, await the outcome with patient resignation. If God sees fit to overcome the evils, cure the illness, or whatever, thank him humbly. But if, on the other hand, he permits the evil to triumph, patiently bless his holy name and surrender yourself to his will for you.[16]

The contemplative stance required by 'ask for nothing, refuse nothing' is also connected with obedience. Obedience in the true sense of the word is about listening. Living this maxim fosters a listening attitude, a disposition of faith, an openness to receive. In no way can it be understood as a law, some external prescription that we are obliged to obey. In the legalist approach to God's will, we can feel safe as long as we are doing what authority tells us to do. A deeper understanding of God's will means that if we are listening to the Spirit in the depths of our being, we will constantly be disturbed out of our comfortable security. This maxim is designed precisely to disturb us.

The obedience required by this maxim is the spirit of the gospel which is a 'new law', a law of the heart. It is an inner law leading us to freedom, allowing ourselves to be drawn, ravished by God.[17] Here we truly enter into the mystery of call and response, our freedom and God's grace that draws us. It is the particular role of the Holy Spirit whose 'inspirations' draw us to this.

Of course, we must emphasise that this maxim, 'ask for nothing, refuse nothing', sounds like absolute madness. It is that gospel foolishness that Paul speaks of, 'fools for Christ'. It only makes sense in the context of a relationship (covenant), otherwise it would be extremely foolish to let go of our securities to trust the other. This is what the maxim invites us to do. It invites us to let go, and to trust that God will provide. It is an act of faith and trust in God and so rests on the belief that God is personable, that God desires to communicate with us, that encounter with God is possible.

If we respond to the invitation, then we are assured that God will provide for us. This is the meaning of the second part of the maxim 'refuse nothing'. Stated positively, this means God will provide for us. However, to arrive at this point we have to take the risk of letting go, handing over, 'asking for nothing'. Now, this will certainly make demands of us. At the level of feeling, it will most certainly feel like surrender. But the other side of the coin of surrender is trust. This is why Francis encourages us constantly to have confidence in the goodness of God. It is to this loving God that we are surrendering, in whom we are placing our trust. It's a way of allowing God to do his part, and therefore

it is an antidote to anxiety. This is the spirit of the beatitudes that
Francis wants to inculcate in us. It is about recognising life as
God's gift and that we are of more value than many sparrows.
God does and will provide for us.

The maxim 'ask for nothing, refuse nothing' is to be lived.
This means that it is not once off, but a lifestyle. It is a discipline
for life. Francis is only too aware of our human weakness. He
uses an image from the writings of Teresa of Avila, who referred
to our mind as an 'unbroken horse', when he says, 'Our horse is
not so well disciplined that we can make him gallop or stop at
will.'[18]

Living the maxim is an on-going discipline that trains us in
the way of surrender and trust. It will lead us to the peace that
Christ promises us, but it will certainly not be arrived at easily:

We do what we can to find the peace of Christ and he does
the rest. But this does not mean that there is no price paid.
Almost certainly we will need to leave behind much that we
have clung to, the familiarity and comfort of being self-suffi-
cient, our reassuring self-confidence, our abounding self-
love. It will be painful. As the scriptures say, to separate us
from our self-love he will bring 'not peace but the sword'.
His sword will leave our hearts raw. We will resist with our
whole being the wrenching that precedes peace. It's true,
however, that in the end, if we remain committed to finding
the will of God, and do our own small bit faithfully and
courageously, he will do the rest. His promised peace will
come. 'Let not my will, but yours be done.' 'Our peace will be
found in the midst of warfare, our serenity will be bought at
the price of surrender.'[19]

'Ask for nothing, refuse nothing', conceived in terms of following the will of God, can be understood as a necessary moment of
waiting. It's the moment of discernment, allowing God's will to
be made manifest. It's a stage in the process. This waiting is essential, but is a prelude to action. Once it becomes clear what the
invitation is, then we are filled with the exuberance of the
beloved in the *Song of Songs* and make haste. We put it into ef-

fect. Having allowed ourselves to be transformed by the love of God, we must not forget that this maxim is not just about me and God. When lived, it leads me necessarily into charitable action. We do not live separate lives. God's transforming action on the individual has an effect on others, because our life is necessarily enmeshed with the lives of others.

Finally, in order to appreciate fully this maxim and prevent it from becoming a distortion of what Francis intended, it is important to bear in mind the following three points:

1. This maxim is to enable us to choose the will of God, therefore, although it seems to demand passivity, there is also an active element to it which demands readiness – it is the biblical demand that we remain awake and watchful. In many ways we are encouraged to live in the season of advent which demands this readiness, this watchfulness.

2. This 'ask for nothing, refuse nothing' is not a permanent state, but a stage in seeking the will of God. Once it becomes clear what the will of God is for us, then we move into action, i.e. Blessed are they who not only hear the word of God, but who keep it.

3. It is precisely in entering into this discernment of God's will that we discover in this in-between stage of 'ask for nothing, refuse nothing', that we receive, not by our own effort but by God's grace, the gift of holy indifference. i.e. a peace of mind and soul (at the supreme point of the spirit, because there can be outward and surface turmoil) that enables us to wait for God's will to manifest itself. But once this becomes clear, then the love that waits (holy indifference) becomes the love which moves us into action (zeal).[20]

It is precisely because of our love for God that we choose 'resignation of our will', that is, abandoning something in favour of somebody – in this case, abandoning our will in favour of God's will. We do this out of love, made possible because of our mutual relationship. If this is not understood, then the giving up of our will/desire would seem to be totally austere, rigorous, something imposed from outside. But if it is seen in the context of a loving union, then, it is seen as a communion of hearts, a communion of wills, a oneness. There are no longer two but one:

> Just as a man on board a ship does not move but lets himself be moved solely by the motion of the vessel in which he is, in like manner the heart that is embarked in the divine good pleasure should have no other will but that of permitting itself to be led by God's will. In such case, the heart no longer says, 'your will be done not mine' for there is no will to renounce. It says these words, 'Lord, into your hands I commend my own will' as though it did not have its will at its own disposal but only at that of divine Providence.[21]

Let us not forget that this invitation to pure love is possible. It is not something we achieve, but rather it is something that God does in and through us. As Francis says in *The Introduction*:

> So God having given us his love, and by it the power and the means to gain ground in the way of perfection, his love does not permit him to let us walk thus alone, but makes him put himself upon the way with us, urges him to urge us, and solicits his heart to solicit and drive forward ours to make good use of the love which he has given us.[22]

CHAPTER EIGHT

Seeking the Will of God

The *will of God* is a term which appears to receive little attention in our modern world. It seems unfashionable. At least, it is a term which has been somewhat silenced. If it does occur in conversation, it is often in a pejorative context. It is seen as an abnegation of responsibility, a fatalistic approach, an infantile passivity. In a world were individualism and autonomy are prized, to speak of God's will is to go against this current. To do so is to return to the *dark ages* where my life is directed from without.

As well as this modern reluctance to de-throne my will in favour of God's will, we need to recognise that the term the *will of God* has a history. It is a central theme in the history of Christian spirituality, tracing its roots to Jesus' own *raison d'être*, 'my food is to do the will of the one who sent me and to complete his work' (Jn 4:34). For Salesian spirituality, any understanding of the will of God must find its source in the person of Jesus. However, the pristine innocence of Jesus' understanding of the will of God has not always travelled well through the course of history. It has received many a distortion on its journey, being used to sanction things which quite clearly were never willed by God. Thus, instead of leading to the freedom that God desires for us, it has been used to burden peoples' lives even further. This is a far cry from the will of God or dream that God has for our world. It is important to note, then, that the *will of God* is not always a neutral term and can conjure up different thoughts and feelings.

Our understanding of the will of God is also very much linked to our image of God. It is important to acknowledge this or else we may very well end up distorting the Salesian understanding of God's will.[1] The Salesian context is a biblical one where God is revealed as love in the person of Jesus Christ. We need to first understand the context. It is not my intention to neutralise the term the *will of God*. It is a term which makes demands of us. However, these demands issue from a loving God. This is why it is necessary to understand the compassion of God as presented in the earlier chapters, before we can begin to respond to the demands of love and compassion that are contained in God's will.

When speaking of the will of God, we need to recognise two freedoms: divine freedom and human freedom. God's ways are not our ways and God is supremely free to act as God chooses. We are free to respond or not, to this divine initiative. We can cooperate with the in-breaking of God's kingdom, sharing in God's creativity, or we can resist and refuse. In short, my will can be in harmony with God's will or not.

In speaking of God's will, Francis is not seeking the extraordinary, but rather, asking us to reflect on our concrete life situation. Indeed, he writes the following:

Everything derives its value from our conformity to God's will; if I am eating or drinking and doing it because God wants me to do it, I am more pleasing to God than if I were to endure death without the intention of doing God's will.[2]

In this respect, small actions are of as much value as heroic actions. The action is evaluated not by its heroism, but rather by its conformity with the will of God. Again and again in Salesian spirituality we will be reminded that we are more likely to meet small occasions in our life where we are asked to do God's will, than await spectacular events.

St Francis de Sales does not offer us a blueprint which maps out God's will for us, but rather offers us important guidelines in seeking to do God's will. It seems to me that we need to grasp these basic tenets if we are to remain on track in discerning the voice of God in our life. Chief among these are the following:
* Fidelity to one's duty
* Living the present moment
* Spiritual direction.

Fidelity to one's duty

An important dimension of Christian spirituality is highlighted by St Francis de Sales, that is the sanctification of work.[3] He is the first to acknowledge that spirituality is not simply the preserve of those in religious life, but is for everyone. It is not a matter of adapting the religious way of life to those living a more 'secular' reality, but rather of finding a spirituality which is at one with their chosen way of life. The will of God is to be discovered precisely in fulfilling our duty. This is the purpose of his *Introduction to The Devout Life*, as he himself writes in the preface:

> My purpose is to instruct those who live in town, within families, or at court, and by their state of life are obliged to live an ordinary life as to outward appearances.[4]

The will of God, therefore, is to be discovered in every state of life. We do not have to wait for the extraordinary to discover its presence, but rather it is in the ordinary routine of our daily life that it is to be discovered. What matters is fidelity to the way of life we are living and avoiding the temptation to fantasise that we would be 'holier' in another way of life. As Francis himself succinctly expresses it, 'of what use is it to build castles in Spain when we must live in France'.[5] Once again Francis calls us back to a spirituality of the real. God's will is to be discovered in what is, not in what we imagine things might be like:

> I can in no way approve that idea that a person obligated to a certain duty or vocation should distract himself by longing for any other kind of life but one in keeping with his duties or by engaging in exercises incompatible with his present state. To do so dissipates his heart and renders it unfit for its needed work. If I want to live the secluded life of the Carthusian, I am wasting my time and such a desire displaces those I should have in order to do good work in my actual state in life.[6]

The real art of the spiritual life is to learn how to move from prayer into our duty, because both are in conformity with God's will:

> You must even accustom yourself to know how to pass from

prayer to all the various duties your vocation and state of life rightly and lawfully require of you ... the lawyer must be able to pass from prayer to pleading cases, the merchant to commerce, and the married woman to her duties as wife and her household tasks, with so much ease and tranquility that their minds are not disturbed.[7]

Indeed, an authentic spiritual life will serve to enrich each person's unique vocation, making 'care of one's family more peaceable, love of husband and wife more sincere, and every type of employment more pleasant and agreeable'.[8] Akin to this is the realisation that each walk of life will present us with many opportunities to transcend ourselves and grow, especially in love for our neighbour. We do not need to go in search of extraordinary penances, but rather respond to the ordinary situations that call us to self-sacrifice:

We would be holy and pleasing to God if we knew how to use well the opportunities of mortifying ourselves that our vocation furnishes us.[9]

To carry out the responsibilities and duties associated with our particular way of life is, for Francis, a concrete way of responding to God's will and a means of living the present moment.

Living the present moment

Do not worry about what will happen tomorrow. The same everlasting Father who cares for you today will take care of you tomorrow and every day. Either he will shield you from suffering or he will give you unfailing strength to bear it.[10]

This classic statement of encouragement to live in the present moment is pivotal in Salesian spirituality. It is something which Francis returns to again and again in his letters of spiritual direction. However, we can also assume that living in the present moment is something which Francis learned from his own painful experience. His adolescent crisis, as examined in the first chapter, taught him the supreme importance of remaining in the present moment:

When our hearts seem to fail us amid fears that arise from

representation of future assaults, it is sufficient to desire courage and trust that God will give it to us at the necessary time.[11]

God's will is to be discovered in the present, but once again the temptation is to dwell on the past or worry about the future. In this respect, anxiety is the biggest threat to living in the present moment and trusting in God. In *The Introduction* he writes that 'with the single exception of sin, anxiety is the greatest evil that can happen to a soul'.[12]

Once again, Francis recalls us to live a spirituality of the real. God's will is discovered in the present moment in what *is,* not in what we imagine or fear. He repeats this again and again to various correspondents:

> Go along with confidence in Divine Providence, worrying only about the present day and leaving your heart in the Lord's love.[13] Live one day at a time, leaving the rest in God's care.[14]

Anxiety robs us of peace of mind and confidence in God. It's as if we become enslaved by worry and caught up in a prison of our own making. The only route of escape is to change our focus from what worries us and turn our focus towards the goodness of God, trusting in his providence. We are asked to do this in the present moment, so that each time the worry surfaces we acknowledge it, but gently turn our focus towards God. In this way, the very thing which seemed to alienate us from God becomes God's point of entry and way of drawing closer to us:

> Our Lord does not want us to ask for our yearly, monthly, weekly bread but our daily bread. Try to do well today without thinking of the following day. Then on the following day try to do the same thing ... Your heavenly Father who has care today will have care tomorrow and after tomorrow, in the measure that, aware of your weakness, you will hope only in his providence.[15]

Another way in which we refuse to remain in the present and, therefore, miss out on God's will for us, is when we desire to be someone else or somewhere else. To want to be something one is not, or to desire to be in a time or place other than the present – neither is possible and neither is the will of God. Thus, both are a simple waste of time and often the cause of our failure to be the saints God wishes us to be.[16]

With his usual wit, Francis writes that at times we can 'imagine we are good angels when we are not even good human beings,' and we can talk eloquently about being spiritual more than translating it into action.[17] It is, therefore, essential to stay with God's will in the present moment. In his *Conferences* to the Visitation Sisters he states:

> If a bishop has the intention to preach a lenten series in a particular diocese and he falls ill and breaks his leg, it is clearly God's will that he not preach the lenten series in that parish, and thus there is no good in worrying about not being able to preach or even regretting it, because it's a sure thing that God wants me to serve him by suffering and not by preaching.[18]

In talking about spirituality in *The Introduction* Francis emphasises that we like to shape it to suit ourselves. This is also true of God's will. In very subtle ways, we can unconsciously try to shape God's will to our own liking. In so doing, these 'empty desires' actually kidnap our awareness from the present moment and the concrete demands of God's will for us:

> If I am sick in bed and yet want to preach, say Holy Mass, visit other sick people, and do the work of healthy persons, are not all these empty desires since it is now beyond my ability to put them into effect? In the meantime these useless desires usurp the place of virtues I ought to have – patience, resignation, mortification, obedience, and meekness under suffering. They are what God wishes me to practice at this time.[19]

It is becoming clearer that the discovery of God's will is very much linked to the concrete situation we find ourselves in. This involves both our duty and the demands of the present moment. We need 'to learn to lay in the manna for each day and no more'.[20] However, given the multitude of conflicting desires we

experience in any given day, how are we to know which to follow and are truly from God? Francis acknowledges that such
discernment necessitates the accompaniment of a good spiritual
director.

Spiritual Direction

'If you wish seriously to travel along the road' of the spiritual
life, then, 'look for a good person to guide and lead you'.[21]

There is an old adage that 'if you have yourself as Master, then
you have a fool for a disciple'. As an astute spiritual director,
Francis recognises that in searching for God's will we can often
be blind or selective in our response. The presence of a director
is essential in challenging any self-delusion on our part, but also
more positively, in helping us to expand our vision. Francis recommends that we pray for a guide, asking God to provide someone who is 'close to his own heart'.[22]

In concrete situations we may experience a conflict of desires
and be unable to truly discern what is God's will. In seeking to
discover God's will, Francis acknowledges that it is not in isol-
ation that we discover it, but through the help of our director.
The director's role is to guarantee that we recognise the good inspirations of God and that we translate these into action at the
appropriate time:

From among all such desires choose, according to your spiritual director's advice, those you can practice and fulfill at present. Turn them to your best advantage, and this done, God
will send you others that you can practice in due time. In this
way you will never waste time in useless desires. I don't say
that you must give up any of these good desires but say that
you must bring them all forth in good order. Those that cannot be immediately put into effect should be stored away in
some corner of your heart until their time comes, and mean-
while you can put into effect the ones that are mature and in
season. I give this advice not only to the spiritual minded but
also to worldly people. Without it we will live only in anxiety
and confusion.[23]

Perhaps the best way of understanding these distinctions is to look at the lived experience of St Jane Frances de Chantal whom Francis helped to steer between these two 'wills' in order to arrive at God's dream for her.

After the death of her husband, Jane Frances had a deep desire to become a religious sister. However, her daily duty as a mother of four children would seem to quite clearly indicate God's will for her. Here we have a clear example of where her desire conflicts with her concrete situation. God seems to be asking one thing of her through her desire and another thing through the concrete situation as widow and mother. What is God's will for her? To pursue the desire and leave her family? Or to let go of her dream to follow God as a sister, and remain a dutiful mother?

As her director, Francis does not rubbish her desire by insisting on her family obligations, but neither does he allow her to yearn ahead of herself or become agitated because she cannot fulfil this desire. He respects both her inner desire and the demands of her family situation. However, he recognises that while her desire is important and authentic, it is not to be realised at present. He does not rule out that it will happen at a later date. For now, however, God's will is to be seen in the demands of family life. Thus, he speaks of the love of submission to God's good pleasure. It's God's good pleasure in this concrete situation that she fulfills the duties and responsibilities to her children. On the other hand, the love of conformity to God's signified will demands that she does not let go of this desire planted within her by God. Hence, to help her in this regard, Francis recommends that when she prays she is to invoke Mary as the abbess of the cloister of her heart. In this way the desire is nurtured through prayer, so that whenever the time is ripe she will be prepared to enter fully into the religious way of life that she has begun to live in her heart. In this way, Francis helps her to steer a path which allows the desire to mature, but at the same time encourages her to respond to her family situation in the present.

THE TWO WILLS OF GOD

It would seem that Francis has managed to synthesise two traditions within the Catholic Church: the monastic, contemplative
tradition with its emphasis on abandonment to God's will, and
the apostolic tradition which has recourse to discernment of
spirits. Francis advocates that we take these two paths in seeking to do God's will. The first he designates as signified *will of
God* and the second as *the will of God's good pleasure*. The first aspect, the *signified will of God* is the interior dimension of
discernment. We have an obligation to discern what is happening within, discerning the 'inspirations' of the Holy Spirit, very
much in keeping with the Jesuitical tradition. Although this is an
interior dimension, it is not just a subjective dimension, because
it involves prayer, scripture, church teaching and spiritual direction. To respond to the *signified will of God* demands the *love of conformity*.

The other pole of discernment is a more objective one described as *the will of God's good pleasure*. This is made manifest in
the circumstances of our lives, especially difficult circumstances
that involve sickness, loss and death. In such painful situations,
it is difficult to understand why such things are allowed, but the
faith required here to follow God's will involves the *love of submission*. These situations call from us a mature faith and deep
trust that God can and does turn everything to good:

> We must have patience not merely at being ill but at having
> the illness that God wishes, where he wishes, among the peo-
> ple he wishes, and with whatever difficulties he wishes. The
> same must be said about other tribulations … When any evil
> happens to you, apply whatever remedies you can and do
> this in a way agreeable to God, since to do otherwise is to
> tempt God. Having done this, wait with resignation for the
> results it may please God to send.[24]

Whenever Francis writes 'let us live courageously between the
one will of God and the other',[25] he is not intending that God has
two wills. God has one will, a dream, a design for us. However,
for us to arrive at this one will we need to take two avenues, as

above, before the two paths become one. We need to take into
account both the signified will of God and the will of God's good
pleasure. This, in turn, requires that we respond with both the
love of conformity and the love of submission. Once again
Francis recommends a spiritual director to accompany us on this
journey, so that we may choose wisely.

CHAPTER NINE

Doing The Will Of God

Love, for Francis de Sales, is not only the goal of the spiritual life but also its starting point. This explains why, as we have already noted, the heart has such a prominent place in the writings and teachings of Francis de Sales. The heart is the source of love and the birthplace of our actions. In keeping with the teachings of Jesus, Francis reminds us of the centrality of our heart:

> The good person out of the good treasure of the heart produces good, and the evil person out of evil treasure produces evil; for it is out of the abundance of the heart that the mouth speaks. (Lk 6:45)

In keeping with the spirit of this scriptural text, Francis writes in the *Introduction* that 'our hearts are trees, affections and passions are branches, and works or actions are fruits … a good tree does not bear anything but good fruit.'[1] It is not our feelings that determine whether we are doing God's will or not, but rather the fruit that our good actions produce. Indeed, Francis continues that good actions 'performed in times of aridity are sweeter and become more precious in God's sight'.[2]

It follows quite naturally for Francis that our actions, then, reveal what state our heart is in. To put it quite simply, what I do reveals who I am. There is a visible relationship between the interior and the exterior. Francis begins with the interior, the heart, but is keen to point out that this leads to the exterior, to action. Love cannot remain just an interior desire but must manifest itself in action. If our compassion and love for others is genuine, then it cannot simply be a desire but must lead to action. The epistle of St James reminds us:

> But someone will say, 'You have faith and I have works.'

> Show me your faith apart from your works, and I by my
> works will show you my faith. (Jas 2:18)

All our acts can and must be inspired by love – this love is always both interior and exterior. Love is concerned with who we are and what we do. Our failure to love can be seen in our neglect or choice not to do something in a concrete situation.

Once we understand this, then it is impossible to distort Salesian spirituality and see it only in terms of an interior reality – it begins with the interior, but must express itself in action. This is evident in God who is love. For Francis, God is this endless creative activity, a movement of love. God's love is revealed first through creation and then through the incarnation. Love is not simply a desire on the part of God, but becomes a reality through God's actions. The supreme expression of God's initiative and action is made visible in the self-sacrifice of Jesus:

> For God so loved the world that he gave his only Son so that
> whoever believes in him should not perish but have eternal
> life.(Jn 3:16)

In giving us his Son, the quality of God's action is love. When we look at the life of Jesus, from a Salesian perspective, we can see his tremendous 'activity'. Francis speaks of the charity practised by Jesus Christ in the whole work of our redemption. We who are called to imitate and follow Jesus are invited into this movement of love. A love which, St Paul points out, not only attracts us but urges us into action, 'the love of Christ urges us' (2 Cor 5:14).

It is now self-evident why we should understand that a Salesian understanding of God's will necessarily lead to action. This is the hallmark of a genuine spirituality which 'consists in a constant, resolute, prompt, and active will to do whatever we know is pleasing to God'.[3] Love, which begins in the heart, expresses itself in action, in doing. The movement of love within God expresses itself in action, culminating in the incarnation where God becomes one of us. Likewise for us, in seeking to do God's will, it begins with the inner movement of love within our heart and necessarily leads to action. Salesian spirituality is an incarnational spirituality because it is intimately involved with this world. It seeks to tune into the movement of God's love within this world and to make God's dream for this world a concrete reality. It is not a flight from the world, rather it is a total immersion in this world. Whilst it does begin with the inner reality of one's heart, it is precisely the conversion of heart that leads to action.

Not only do Francis's writings attest to this, but we must never forget the witness of his life, of his activity, of his love which expresses itself in action. He is intensely engaged in public life as a bishop of his diocese, spiritual director, preacher, writer, correspondent with people in all walks of life. Born into a noble family and university educated in law, theology, philosophy and rhetoric, Francis is nevertheless one of the people. In imitation of the good shepherd, he spends himself tirelessly for his flock, especially those on the margins of society.

His understanding of God as love is not some intellectual notion, but is given concrete expression in his love for the poor. From his earliest days his mother inculcated in him a love for the poor. This predilection for the poor finds expression from the very beginning of his pastoral activity. He requests to go on a mission in the Chablais region, fraught with dangers and hardships. Here he 'will learn what the rough life in a fortress is like. He will live in a little dark room, in which there will probably be no candle; some days he will have to share a soldier's shelter, Nicot's, and not have a minute's solitude'.[4] In communion with the poor, he will preach by example. He will sleep on bare boards most of the time. He will find himself in such poverty-stricken places that they will only be able 'to receive him in a wretched manner ... but among smiling happy faces, it was really a delight to him to suffer discomfort'.[5]

Indeed, by ministering to the poor, Francis is ministered to by them. Through their poverty he will discover a God 'full of gentleness and tenderness in the midst of these towering harsh mountains where many simple souls dearly love him, really and sincerely, and for this God, deer and chamois were leaping here and there over the terrible ice, proclaiming his praises'.[6] Francis had only one unique model in his apostolate by personal contact – the itinerant Jesus. On principle he usually travelled on foot so that he could meet the poor and enter into personal contact with them. His valet, Germain Pilliod, attests to this love of the poor, declaring that 'the space around his confessional began to resemble the rendezvous of the poor, the beggars, the most repulsive, the deaf, those with ulcers and infectious diseases, foul-smelling wretches rejected by other confessors; they found in the bishop one who showed them great satisfaction'.[7] Furthermore, he expressly forbade that any beggar should be turned away from his door, and when disobeyed on this point, he could be 'most unpleasant'.[8]

The gentle and humble Francis did not mince his words when it came to condemning injustice and the exploitation of the poor. From the pulpit he reprimanded those who were using war to 'grow richer and fatter' while others 'were reduced to beggary'.[9]

Similarly, he fought the lust for wealth among the clergy. It was a time when most of the clergy led the life of feudal lords, wealthy landowners, warriors, diplomats or even elegant courtiers. Francis chose to be poor and to remain poor. In contrast to the ostentatious display of wealth by many bishops, Francis's idea of a bishop's glory was to follow Christ in his poverty. 'He therefore kept as few people as possible in his retinue, no carriage, no valets, one cook, one lackey and at the very beginning a secretary and a tailor who turned his old cassocks into underwear.'[10] He refused a purseful of gold crowns offered by the Duchess de Longueville; he declined the offer of the king of the first vacant bishopric in France 'which would be worth four times that of Geneva'.[11] Such facts speak louder than words. Francis believed that the love of money was the most virulent form of selfish love:

> You cannot serve two masters ... if you hold yourself in contempt, he taught, you would also hold wealth in contempt.[12]

Such a disinterested zeal as displayed by Francis was practically unknown among the clergy. This rigorous kenosis in his pastoral activity and the embracing of poverty, bespeak his belief in the preferential love of God for the poor.

ST JOHN BOSCO

Almost two hundred years later, a young peasant boy born John Melchior Bosco, was to become one of Francis's most famous disciples. Inspired by the spirituality of St Francis, he was to give a unique expression of this spirituality of gentleness and love in his response to the young, especially the poorest of them.[13] Unlike his patron, John Bosco was born into a peasant family, lost his father at a very early age and was forced to leave home when still quite young. With the loss of both father and home, the young John Bosco could have retreated from the world and raised a wall of defences around himself. He chose another way. Despite his suffering and loss, he allowed his already wounded heart to be expanded by God – he chose to give. He gave abundantly without counting the cost. He grappled with his own loss around fatherhood and home, and opened his heart to become a father for the young and to provide a home for them.

Turin, with its rapid industrialisation was a place teeming with young people, uprooted from home, from the country, without family or a place to stay. Many of these young people became involved in petty crime and ended up in prison. On visiting these prisons, John Bosco realised more and more that this could be prevented, if the young people had a friend who would be genuinely interested in them and mentor them. This pragmatic spirituality he later called the 'preventive system' which was based on reason, religion and loving kindness in imitation of St Francis de Sales.[14]

John Bosco began his work of gathering young people together, meeting them on their territory so that the playground soon became his parish. He had tremendous difficulty trying to get a place that he and his young people could call home. They had to wander from place to place, always being moved on. It is extremely significant that when he eventually manages to find a place it is situated on the outskirts of the city. He is pushed to the very edges, the margins, because of his association with the homeless young people. In him the drama of the incarnation is repeated – there is no room at the inn, he came among his own and his own received him not (Jn 1:11). It is not by accident that he names this place the Oratory of St Francis de Sales.[15]

From these humble beginnings, the religious order founded by St John Bosco has grown prodigiously. The 'worker priest', as John Bosco has been described,[16] emphasised shortly before his death at his last General Chapter that the Salesian Congregation would flourish only if it remained faithful to the spirit of St Francis de Sales. In one of his letters to the Salesians he writes:

> I would like to give a sermon to all of you or better a conference on the Salesian Spirit which must animate and direct all our activities and the accomplishment of our duties. The preventive system is something which is our very own ... Every Salesian should be a friend to all; he must never seek revenge; he should be quick to pardon and should not drag up things that have already been pardoned ... Gentle kindness in speaking and in helping others wins over all hearts.[17]

The life of St John Bosco is characterised by the same zeal as Francis, a restless activity on behalf of the young and the poor. Like Francis, his pastoral concern is that of the Good Shepherd. In the commentary on the Salesian Constitutions it says:

> Here we see the preoccupation of the Good Shepherd who *wins hearts by gentleness and self-giving*. 'I am the good shepherd. The good shepherd lays down his life for the sheep.'(Jn 10:11)[18]

This is a reminder of the kindness and gentleness characteristic of the Salesian spirit,[19] even at the cost of self-denial. From his dream at the age of nine, Don Bosco had learned 'not by blows but by love and gentleness must you win friends...'[20] 'Do not forget the importance of gentleness in our actions; win over the hearts of the young by means of love; remember that saying of St Francis de Sales: "more flies are caught with a cup of honey than with a barrel of vinegar".'[21]

Gentleness is at the core of the Salesian spirit – and this can only be achieved at a cost because it demands an ocean of patience. It involves a real death to self, to one's ego. As Don Bosco says himself in one of his letters:

> How often in my long career has this great truth come home to me! It is so much easier to get angry than to be patient, to threaten a boy rather than to persuade him. I would even say that usually it is so much more convenient for our own impatience and pride to punish them than to correct them patiently and with firmness and gentleness.[22]

Don Bosco, inspired by Francis, chose one of his maxims as the motto of the Salesian congregation:

> Give me people (souls), take everything else …[23]

It is about salvation. It is about being saved. And here we are not just talking about the next life, we are talking about the here and now. We are talking about the quality of life we have here and now. God desires that we have fullness of life, and is restless until we receive it. In many parts of our world there are people deprived of their human dignity; how can our hearts be at rest as long as this is happening?

What is the source of this motto?[24] In Genesis 14:21 we have the story of the people being captured and Abraham has to rescue them by night. When he wins, he says to the other kings ,'You can have the booty, all the treasure. What I want is the people.' He redeems them, he buys their freedom. This theme is repeated throughout the Old Testament because it is the primary experience of the people of Israel – they begin in slavery and are freed. Abraham, in this sense, mirrors the activity of God which is to release from oppression.

This role performed by Abraham became known as the GO-EL.[25] Jesus is the *Goel*, the one who delivers from bondage, oppression, the one who redeems. The person of Jesus clearly mirrors the restless heart of God who seeks to liberate and bring to fullness of life. It is this activity, movement, restlessness of the heart of God that inspires both St Francis de Sales and St John Bosco. They enter into the movement of this restlessness of God's heart through their pastoral activity. It is a love which is both affective and effective because it takes into account the salvation of the whole person.

The Ecstasy of Action

What must be kept in mind is that although Francis begins with the interior, the will, he is keen to point out that the will leads to action and, therefore, love cannot remain just an interior desire but must manifest itself in action. There is a visible relationship between the interior and the exterior – what I do reveals who I am. 'Let your actions be like clear water so that people can see your heart from where they arise.' Salesian spirituality is concerned with all our acts. No act is trivial in itself. All our acts can and must be inspired by love – this love is always both 'affective and effective', 'interior and exterior'.

This truth is encapsulated in the Salesian dictum 'set me like a seal on your heart and a seal on your arm', taken from the *Song of Songs*. What does Francis mean by this, but that true, authentic spirituality is one of love which manifests itself in action. Our good intention is not enough; we need to translate it into action. This is why Francis is very wary about those who see spirituality merely in terms of an altered state of consciousness or of feeling good. We may not be able to control how we feel, but we can control how we choose to act. We do not have to *feel loving* to do the loving thing. Feeling good or having some extraordinary *religious* experience is not the criterion to judge the authenticity of one's spirituality. As if to ground us, Francis reminds us that it is not the flight of mystical experiences that guarantee holiness, but rather doing the loving thing. Therefore, it is the person whom we love least that challenges us to love, rather than any mystical feelings we may have. In this respect he is very much in harmony with St Teresa of Avila who reiterates that it is not *mystical experiences* which are the guarantee of holiness, but good works.[26]

Salesian mysticism, then, is this synthesis of the interior life and action, and love is the principle that unites both the interior and exterior, the affective and effective, contemplation and action:

AFFECTIVE	EFFECTIVE
In the first of these ways we grow fond of God, of what he likes.	In the second we serve God and do what he commands.
The first way unites us with God's goodness.	The second urges us to carry out his will.
In the first we find God pleasing.	In the second he is pleased with us.
In the first way we clasp God to our heart in loving embrace.	In the second we carry him in our arms by the practice of virtue.[27]

Once we understand this, then it is impossible to distort Salesian Spirituality and see it only in terms of an interior reality – it begins with the interior, but must express itself in action.

> I cannot approve the methods of those who try to reform a person by beginning with outward things, such as bearing, dress or hair. On the contrary, it seems to me that we ought to begin inside. 'Be converted to me with your whole heart,' God said. 'My son, give me your heart.' Since the heart is the source of all our actions, as the heart is so are they.[28]

Love is ecstatic, goes out of itself, is characterised by movement, activity. When Francis de Sales talks of love, it is not a sentiment but the act of loving that he is dealing with. Although the word love is over-used and can be misinterpreted, a reality even in Francis's day, he still prefers to use it than other terms like, for example, dilection:

> The word 'love' signifies greater fervour, efficacy, and activity than does dilection … and it is because I intend to speak of the acts of charity rather than of charity as a habit. (I,14, p 395)

We need only recall the first pages of the *Treatise* to see the activity, the movement, of God who is love at work in our universe. We are called, through love, to enter into this movement of love. Jesus is the supreme expression of God's activity, God at work in our universe. When we look at the life of Jesus, from a Salesian perspective, we can see his tremendous 'activity'.

Francis speaks of the charity practised by Jesus Christ in the whole work of our redemption.[29]

The key to understanding this dynamic of love that not only attracts us, but also urges us into action, is to be found in the Pauline text 2 Cor 5:14. After quoting this, he continues: 'the holy love of the Saviour presses us ... like a vine to an elm, to enable it in some way to participate in his fruit ...'[30] It is Jesus, the only Son of the Father, the beloved, beautiful amongst all the children of men, who is able to worthily lend praise to God. 'Only God can give to God the praise which is his due.' It is by entering into this mystery, becoming the body of Christ, that we give God the praise that is his due. This action comes about through the activity of God:

> Sometimes it seems that we begin to join and attach our-
> selves to God even before he joins himself to us. This is be-
> cause we perceive the unitive action on our part without per-
> ceiving what God is doing on his part. However, there is no
> doubt that his action always precedes ours, although we do
> not always perceive his previous action. He always chooses
> us and takes hold of us before we choose him or take hold of
> him.[31]

For Francis de Sales, the apostolate is rooted in praise. If the love of complacence draws the perfections of God into our heart, the love of benevolence makes our heart go out of itself to praise God and to work for his glory.

CHAPTER TEN

Joy and Optimism

Consistently in the writings of St Francis de Sales we have the idea that happiness or true joy is a fruit of living a life which is in accord with the will of God. We have seen how he held a special place in the lives of many in their discernment of what God was calling them to. His genius lay in seeing that discernment was not simply avoiding temptations and doing ascetical practices, but rather that it was important to identify good desires that were not to be suppressed. If these good desires could not be realised immediately because of circumstances, nevertheless they were to be maintained and cultivated so that they could be fulfilled in accord with God's plan:

> God knows why he permits so many good desires to be realised only after such a long time and so much suffering, and sometimes they cannot be realised at all. When no other benefit is derived from this except the mortification of souls who love him, that is still a great deal. In a word, one should never desire anything evil, want good things slightly, but desire without out measure the divine good which is God.[1]

Joy is the fruit of a virtuous life. It does not mean that we are free of all suffering, but rather that even in the midst of trials there is a deeper reality when we are at peace with God and our neighbour. Often people seek joy through pleasure and while the two are not unrelated, they are very different. Pleasure is transient, joy is not simply a feeling but the fruit of a 'rightly ordered life, moving in a positive direction that makes us happy on the surface and gives a deep inner contentment'.[2] What we are speaking of is integrity – when there is a consistency between my words and actions, when what I do confirms who I am. The fruit of such a lifestyle is the beatitude of joy.

When we live a life consistent with our vocation, rooted in confidence and trust in God, it produces a deep serenity. It is when we are at odds with the deepest desires of our heart and what God wills for us, that we lose our way. However, God's inspirations are always calling us back to our heart and to himself where he dwells within our heart. God knows us better than we know ourselves and so, our hope lies in God's knowledge of us:

> God alone by his infinite knowledge sees, searches, and penetrates all the twists and turns of our minds. He understands our 'thoughts from afar'. He discovers our paths, doubling back, and evasive turns. His knowledge of all this is wonderful; it surpasses our powers and we cannot attain to it ... [3]

God understands only too well our human weakness and so he provides for us, constantly meeting our unfaithfulness with his fidelity. He provides an infinite way of healing and nourishing us, especially the classical means for Christian perfection, such as prayer and the sacraments. While our effort in attaining Christian perfection is important, Francis emphasises the centrality of love. Of primary importance, then, is friendship with God. Consequently, the road to sanctity does not consist in perfecting oneself, but in loving. It is this pathway that leads to our happiness and makes our joy complete:

> Such is my beloved, and he is the friend of my heart ... My God is so rich in all that is good and that his goodness is so infinite and his infinity so good.[4]

Herein lies the source of our joy and hope, the goodness of God. In acknowledging this fundamental truth, we can conclude with confidence that God who is good has created us good. Our heart is made for the heart of God:

> As soon as we give a little attentive thought to the divinity we feel a certain sweet emotion within our heart, and this testifies that God is God of the human heart ... This pleasure, this confidence that our heart naturally has in God, assuredly comes from nowhere but the congruity existing between God's goodness and our soul.[5]

OPTIMISM AND CHRISTIAN HUMANISM

Christian humanism lies at the basis of Salesian optimism.[6] Francis recognises the existence of original sin and also the weakness of fallen humanity, but never forgets the possibility of grace. Despite the prodigal nature of our heart, at the core of our being we are being called back to the true, the beautiful, the good. God is calling us back and is always present in our heart even when we have turned away. Francis writes:

> Have your ever seen a large fire covered over with ashes? Ten or twelve hours later when someone comes looking for fire, he finds a little in the centre of the hearth and even that little is found with difficulty. Yet, there it was, since it is found there, and from it he can again light up the other coals which had died out. It is the same with charity, our spiritual life, in the midst of great violent temptations … yet in spite of all the trouble and disorder we feel in both soul and body it is really there.[7]

In harmony with Christian humanism, the theology of Francis de Sales greatly emphasises the effects of our redemption: 'Just as there is no natural temperament so good that it may not be perverted by bad habits, so there is no natural temperament so difficult that it may not be overcome with care and perseverance and the grace of God.'[8] He goes so far as to say: 'Our Saviour's redemption touches our distress and makes it more worthwhile, more lovable, than ever original innocence could have been.'[9]

The source of our optimism lies in what God has provided through his providence, both natural and supernatural. Francis returns to the image of Jacob's ladder to paint a picture of the devout life, lived for God, that will bring joy and happiness. In keeping with the tradition of the Fathers of the church, Francis sees in this image a sign of the providential care God exercises on earth through the ministry of angels. He also recognises in it a foreshadowing of the incarnation of the Word who linked heaven with earth. These two aspects of providential care and the incarnation are present in Francis' use of the image:

> On the Saviour's redemption is based the whole mystical lad-

der of that greater Jacob, both at its end in heaven, since it
rests on the loving bosom of the eternal Father, and at its end
on earth, since it is planted in the bosom and pierced side of
our Saviour, who for this cause died on Mount Calvary.[10]

In this we can see the source of our joy and optimism because
God remains faithful and provides for us despite our infidelity.
Even after Adam's sin, God willed that all people be saved, in
such a way that they maintained their freedom. To help us on
the journey to salvation, God provides us with grace so that we
might become what we are created for. Since we are free, we can
resist this grace, but God continues to provide for those who
turn away through penitence.

Francis makes use of the image of Jacob's ladder to communicate this simple yet profound reality that God provides for us
the means that lead to our salvation:

> Jacob's ladder is an excellent picture of the devout life, the
> life lived for God. The two uprights represent prayer, which
> obtains for us the love of God, and the sacraments which confer
> it. The rungs of the ladder are the steps of love. On these, one
> descends by action to help and support one's neighbour, or
> ascends by contemplation to loving union with God ... Those
> on the ladder have beautiful and cheerful faces because they
> receive all things with happiness and contentment.[11]

It will only be in the next life that we will fully appreciate what
God has done for us, how he 'led, drew and carried us on the
way'. We will confess that we owe all our happiness to the Lord
'since he has done for us all that Jacob, the great patriarch, desired for his journey when he saw the ladder to heaven':

> Lord you were with me and you guided me on the way by
> which I came hither. You gave me the bread of the sacra-
> ments for food. You clothed me with the wedding garment of
> charity. You have happily led me to this mansion of glory
> which, O my Father eternal, is your home.[12]

Our hope, our joy, our happiness consists in this reality that we
are made for God and we will be united with God one day. As
Francis himself remarks, 'Note well how ardently God desires

us to be his, since to this end he has made himself entirely ours.' Francis returns constantly to the marvel of the incarnation – wondering at the lengths to which God has been prepared to go to in order to achieve our happiness:

> The cross is the root of every grace received by us who are spiritual grafts engrafted on his body. Having been so en-grafted, if we abide in him, then by means of the life of grace he will communicate to us we shall certainly bear the fruit of glory prepared for us.[13]

Francis acknowledges that this destiny of happiness with God is not merited by us, but pure gift. Nevertheless he says, 'For although to belong to God is a gift from God, yet it is a gift that God denies no one.'[14]

SADNESS AND JOY

Can we say that the life lived by Jesus contained no sadness? I think not, but Francis is keen to point out that there are different types of sadness which we will examine later. If this is so, should we expect the lives of those who follow Jesus to be without sad-ness? Before the coming of the Spirit the element of sadness is quite present in the liturgy – the followers of Jesus are full of sadness at the imminent departure of Jesus which is necessary. He reminds us that we will have sorrow at the passing of the old, but this will give way to joy when we experience the life of the Spirit:

> In a short time you will no longer see me, and then a short time later you will see me again ... You will be weeping and wailing while the world will rejoice; you will be sorrowful, but your sorrow will turn to joy ... so it is with you now: You are sad now, but I shall see you again, and your hearts will be full of joy, and that joy no one shall take from you ... (Jn 16:19-22)

Francis does go on to distinguish between different types of sad-ness, quoting St Paul, 'For the sadness which is according to God leads to repentance and then to salvation with no regrets; it is the world's kind of sadness that ends in death' (2 Cor 7:10). He continues by illustrating various figures who exhibited this 'sadness according to God' – David, St Peter, Magdalen who wept over their sins; Jeremiah wept over the ruin of Jerusalem, Our Lord over the Jews ... In another place, he states 'the sadness of true penance does not so much deserve the name of sadness as of displeasure against sin'.

However, there is a sadness of this world which proceeds from three causes:

1. A temptation to despair which has evil as its source and whose aim is to disturb our spirit. Laying an ambush in sadness, this is quickly followed by a multitude of distressing thoughts which lead to doubts, jealousies, aversions and a variety of vain, bitter and melancholy subtleties, in order that we may reject all kinds of reasons and consolations.[15]

2. Sadness proceeds at other times from our natural condition, when the melancholic humour predominates within us – this is not evil in itself, but evil can make use of it to brew a thousand temptations in our souls, e.g. for as spiders only make their webs when the weather is dark and cloudy, so too can the forces of evil find no better time to lay their snares.[16]

3. There are external circumstances which bring sadness upon us: e.g. the death of someone we love, cf. Jacob at the news of the death of Joseph, David at the death of Absalom. Such sadness is common to both the good and the bad, but with the good it is moderated by acquiescence and resignation to God's will, cf. Tobias who, for all the adversities that befell him, returned thanks to God, and in Job, who blessed the name of the Lord for afflictions, and in Daniel, who changed his sorrows into canticles.[17]

St Francis did not want people to be sad: 'Strive to overcome all melancholy feelings and all sadness. Try to live in peace.'[18] He wanted people to be always joyful: 'The Israelites were never able to sing in Babylon because they kept thinking of their homeland, but I want us to sing everywhere.'[19]

As an astute spiritual director, Francis noted that often the cause of our sadness is due to an unhealthy preoccupation with our weaknesses and sinfulness. He writes to Jane de Chantal:

... in short, I am as much yours as you could ever wish me to

JOY AND OPTIMISM   115

be: Guard yourself against anxiety, depression, scruples. You
would never in the world want to offend God; that is reason
enough to live joyously.[20]

In a letter to Madame de la Flèchere, he writes, 'Maintain a spirit
of holy joy which, in a quiet way, will effect your words and
deeds so that God may be given the glory when people see
you.'[21] Even more tellingly he declares to Soeur de Blonay,
novice mistress at Lyons:

> Our imperfections must not give us pleasure ... But neither
> must they astonish us nor take away our courage. We must,
> indeed, draw from them submission, humility and distrust of
> ourselves, but not discouragement, nor affliction of heart,
> much less distrust of the love of God towards us. So God
> does not love our imperfections and venial sins, but he loves
> us greatly in spite of them ... Live joyously. Our Lord watches
> over you, and watches over you with love, and with greater
> tenderness insofar as you have more infirmity.[22]

Not only does he not permit people to be overwhelmed by sadness, but he also encourages people to stir up in their hearts the
joy that gushes forth from a life lived in Christ. 'Live joyfully in
that divine Jesus who is King of angels and of men; the joy that
comes from our belonging to God and the adhesion of our wills
to his. God makes us his alone, because only then shall we be
happy; everything else is nothing but vanity and affliction of
spirit.'[23] Of course Francis is realistic enough to recognise that
we are not always in control of our moods and we cannot 'be
cheerful at will. However, it is inexcusable for us not to be pleasant, agreeable and considerate at all times.'[24]

The devotion desired by Francis was not one of sadness, suited
only to melancholy people. He condemns those who promoted
this type of devotion:

> O these preachers! They forbid every joy, every tasty morsel,
> every smile, any concern for temporal goods. They want you to
> spend all day in church, always to be fasting. They are traitors
> to humanity! We do not say these things, but 'Enjoy every
> pleasure, but sinful pleasure, never.'[25]

Francis emphasises the light that comes to us from the natural inclination to love God, directing us along the right path. This too is a joy and delight because 'it gives us confidence that God, who leaves in us the imprint of this wondrous seal, the symbol of our origin, also means to bring, to drive us home to him if only we are fortunate enough to allow ourselves to be captivated by his goodness'.[26]

Anxiety tries to rob us of joy, which is also why he advises us not to torment ourselves over our defects, but to 'walk simply in the way of the Lord' for there is nothing like fretfulness and anxiety over your defects to preserve them and make it difficult to remove them. He applies to himself what he counsels to others:

> I know what sort of being I am; yet even though I feel myself miserable, I am not troubled at it; rather I am sometimes joyful at it, considering that I am a truly fit object for the mercy of God, to which I continually recommend you.[27]

Francis himself was well able to lead people to a state of tranquility and encouragement, precisely because of his own experience. He knew what it was to suffer depression as he himself had been obliged to pass through the severest trials, and arrived at the possession of peace of heart only by a total abandonment to God:

> Since at every season of life, early or late, in youth or in old age, I can expect my salvation from the pure goodness and mercy of God alone, it is much better to cast myself from this moment into the arms of his mercy than to wait till another time.[28]

We cannot engraft an oak on a pear tree, so contrary are these two trees to each other. We can no more engraft sadness or despair unto charity.[29] How can sadness be useful to holy charity, since among the fruits of the Holy Spirit, joy holds the very next place to charity.

CHAPTER ELEVEN

Friendship in Salesian Spirituality

Faithful friends are a sturdy shelter:
whoever finds one has found a treasure.
Faithful friends are beyond price;
no amount can balance their worth;
Faithful friends are life-saving medicine;
and those who reverence God will find them.
Those who reverence God direct their friendship aright,
for as they are, so are their neighbours also.[1]

Francis believes that we do not have two hearts, one to love God and one to love our neighbour. It is his genius to perceive that we do not come to God bypassing the things and persons that God has created, but rather through them. True love of another is not a hindrance to our love of God. The two loves, divine and human, are intimately intertwined. We learn to love both God and others at the same time. It is as if our hearts undergo an expansion in the very process of loving itself. In the material world when we give we have less; in the spiritual world another law operates: it is in giving that we receive, it is in loving that our capacity for love grows, it is not lessened but increased.

HUMAN AND DIVINE FRIENDSHIP

True friendship is liberating for friends and is truly a gift from God. It enables each person to grow in his or her own identity and become the person he or she is called to be. Indeed, Francis recommends such friendships as being necessary for our growth on our spiritual journey:

Many people say, 'We should not have any particular friendship or affection since it fills our hearts, distracts our minds and causes envy.' But for those who live in the world and desire to embrace true virtue it is necessary to unite together in holy, sacred friendship. By this means they encourage, assist and lead one another to perform good deeds.[2]

Indeed, Francis understands the very nature of the church in terms of such friendship.[3] It is the gathering of friends who live with one heart, one mind and one soul. This communitarian aspect of the church mirrors the heart of God which is community. We can even say that 'the trinitarian life can be called "ecclesial" because all of its activity depends on a communitarian life of love between persons who communicate to each other all their perfection, their very nature, without diminishing in any way their personality, their identity'.[4]

In earlier chapters, we have noted that there exists a friendship within God which is beyond comparison.

... if friendship is a thing to be loved and longed for, whose friendship can be such in comparison with that infinite friendship which is between the Father and the Son.[5]

What is essential to this friendship is what is communicated: 'From all eternity there is in God an essential communication by which the Father, in producing the Son, communicates his entire, infinite and indivisible divinity to the Son. The Father and the Son together, in producing the Holy Spirit, communicate in like manner their own proper unique divinity to him.'[6] Thus, the ecstatic giving of love totally to the other is then communicated to creation. This is true of God, but also of us who are created in his image and likeness. We can only realise this image of God in ourselves whenever we likewise go out in love. He attests to this truth in his first sermon where he says:

The creation of the universe introduces the divine majesty in three persons, when he says: 'Let us make man to our likeness!' (Gen 1:26); for if only one person had created man, he would have said: 'I make', and not 'Let us make', as we find written ...'[7]

It follows that to realise the divine image within us we can only do so in relation to God and to others. Friendship calls us to this. We exercise friendship in charity when we respond with a love of benevolence for our neighbour, seeking nothing for ourselves. In spiritual friendships, however, there is a mutuality in which we both give and receive love, helping the other and ourselves to realise the divine image within us.

The scandal of division within the church is precisely a failure to recognise this truth, that we are called to be one body in Christ. To one of his correspondents he writes:

> The children of this world are all separated one from another because their hearts are in different places; but the children of God whose hearts are where their treasure is and who all have the same treasure – which is the same God – are consequently always bound and united together.[8]

Francis, living at the time of religious wars, is only too aware of the scar this creates on the communal body. It is at odds with the early church where they live with one heart and one soul. The true nature of the church is 'made up of people assembled by the word of God, called into existence by love and maintained in existence by love, which is the true "cement that holds together the living stones of the church".'[9]

Spiritual Friendships:

It is quite clear to Francis that the Holy Spirit is the author of *spiritual friendships*, because it is the Spirit who creates, nurtures and sustains such friendships. In a letter to one of his directees he writes: 'It is the Spirit of God who is the author of the holy friendship which we have for each other'.[10] Distance, or being separated, is no obstacle to such a friendship. The main aim of such friendships is to help us on our spiritual journey, to become closer to each other and to God. As he himself eloquently writes, a spiritual friendship is that 'by which two, three or more souls share their devotion and spiritual affection, and establish a single spirit among themselves'.[11]

As the author of spiritual friendships, the Holy Spirit reveals the qualities of such friendships.[12] The qualities that we cherish in human friendship are to be discovered in scriptures as having their source in the Holy Spirit. It is the Spirit of God who leads us into love (1 Jn 4:13):

* a friend loves (Rom 5:5)
* a friend forgives (Jn 20:22-23)
* a friend shares secrets (Jn 15:15)
* a friend speaks on our behalf (Mt 10:20)
* a friend delights in being with the other (Acts 9:31)
* a friend respects another's freedom (2 Cor 3:18)
* a friend is like another self (Eph 1:13)
* a friend bestows gifts (1 Cor 12:8-11)
* a friend seeks the good of the other (Rom 8:13).

As well as being our helper and our guide, the Spirit is also our friend. It is the Spirit who draws us into friendships which promote our human and spiritual growth. In a very real way, we can speak of friendship as being a sacrament of God's presence.

Francis writes:
> Friendship requires close communication between friends, since otherwise it can neither come into existence nor remain in existence.[13]

As well as the need for communication, the nature of the friendship is determined by what is communicated. 'According to the diversity of communications, friendship also differs, and the communications differ according to the variety of the goods that they communicate to each other.'[14] So if two people love each other, know about their love but do not communicate, there is love but no friendship. In his view '... friendship is the most dangerous love of all because the other loves can exist without intercommunication, but friendship is completely based on it, and we can hardly have such communication with a person without sharing this person's qualities'.[15]

If what is communicated is evil, vain and frivolous, then the friendship is evil, vain and frivolous. For a true and genuine friendship to exist, something good has to be communicated. The higher and more noble this good is, the more noble the friendship will be. The best kind of friendship is the one in which 'mutual and reciprocal communications spring from charity, devotion, and Christian perfection ...':

> O God, how precious this friendship will be! It will be excellent because it comes from God, excellent because it leads to God, excellent because its bond will endure eternally in God. How good it is to love here on earth as they love in heaven and to learn to cherish one another in this world as we shall do eternally in the next.[16]

This is what is known as a spiritual friendship. Such an idea is also to be found in the Irish tradition of soul friend (*anam chara*).

Francis does not, as we see from above, canonise friendship *per se*. It is what is communicated in the friendship that is of supreme importance. If virtues are communicated, then that friendship is to be commended, especially if it involves the virtues of prudence, discretion, fortitude, justice etc. leading to charity, the bond of perfection.[17] Friendships, therefore, are not only a means of support but they shape us as well. He warns against 'phantom friendships', ones which do not truly deserve the name of friendship.[18] He says we are easily attracted to people because of external beauty, pleasing characteristics or accomplishments, wishing that we ourselves could have these things. However, such friendships can be vain and frivolous,. As he says himself, 'In a word, they are the sport of courts but not of hearts.'[19] These reflections are obviously based on his own experience of life at the court.

SOUL-FRIENDS: FRANCIS AND JANE

Among the many letters of spiritual direction written by Francis, the ones written to Jane Frances de Chantal, above all, reveal the fruitfulness of an authentic spiritual friendship.[20] They are letters full of warmth, self-revelation and mutual respect.[21] In a moving passage to St Jane de Chantal he writes:

> '... there is no soul in the world, it seems to me, that loves more affectionately, more tenderly and, to say it once and for all, more lovingly than I. For it pleased God to make my heart this way.'

However, this does not mean that he is given to a saccharine sentimentality, for he hastens to add:

> 'But nonetheless, I love independent and vigorous souls who are not too sentimental. For an excessive tenderness confounds the heart, disquiets it and distracts it from affectionate prayer toward God (and) hinders complete resignation and the death of self-love ...'[22]

When Francis meets Jane de Chantal, she is a woman who has already experienced the trauma of losing her husband and is immersed in the task of raising her children. At Dijon, she has already been directed by the Carmelites for four years. Thus, in a real sense, she comes to Francis already formed and, although she will receive much under his direction, she will also bestow much on him.

At one point, early in the friendship, he asks Jane if she wants to marry again. She declares not, and he makes a quip about her attire, 'you should pull down the flag then!' Within months of their first meeting, Francis writes to her:

> ... from the very first time that you consulted me about your interior life, God granted me a great love for your spirit. When you confessed to me in greater detail, a remarkable bond was forged in my soul that caused me to cherish your soul more and more ...[23]

Speaking of Jane, Francis alludes to the text in Gen 2:8 and calls her a 'help' in the spiritual life and in the foundation of the Visitation:

> 'Our Lord gave me a help who not only is similar to me but who is so like me that she and I are one spirit.'[24] Not only one spirit, but also one heart with her: 'This sacred fire which changes all into itself, wants to transform our hearts so that there be only love and we be no longer loving but love; no longer two, but only one, since love unites all things in sovereign unity.'[25]

According to the editors of his *Oeuvres*, through his contact with Jane 'he experiences to a supreme degree divine love; both help each other, sustain each other, stimulate each other, drawing close to the eternal hearth of their friendship, in which they were a pure radiance for each other'.[26] It is she who initiates him into the mysteries of Carmelite spirituality, as Bremond says: 'He had entrusted himself to her as a novice as regards St Teresa. She professed him.'[27] This will have a profound effect not only on his writing of the *Treatise of the Love of God*, but an important stage in the development of his own mystical journey.

As a directee of Francis, Jane enlightened him as regards what was happening in himself. Furthermore, in directing her, he was enabled to understand the different ways in which God works in the soul. The aridities that she experienced helped him not to stop at the gentleness that he was experiencing himself. As Wright says:

> The geography of Francis' ongoing relationship with the divine and the vistas of self that he experienced in pursuing that relationship were, on the whole, like broad plateaus and open prairies. There is a certain sense of freedom and spaciousness, a view of wide horizons and the feel of light about him. For Jane, the relationship with the divine was mapped with deep valleys and cavernous places; the darkness of her inner landscape with its trials, temptations, anguish and uncertainty seems to be punctuated only by periodic emergences into the fresh air and light of mountain heights.[28]

It is clear that both Francis and Jane are marked by different temperaments and personal history. Grief and loss is very much a part of her life which accounts for her inner exodus of suffering which lasted for more than forty years. In writing his *Treatise*[29] Francis composes a parable of a deaf musician which is really the story of Jane's interior struggle:

> I am working on your ninth book of *The Love of God:* Praying today before my crucifix, God has shown me your soul and your state by comparing them to an excellent musician ... the poor musician became deaf like you, and could no longer hear his own music. His master was often absent, but he kept on singing because he knew his master had taken him on to sing.[30]

Their friendship allowed for the on-going discernment of what God was doing in their lives and what God was calling them to beyond the relationship. One notable occasion was Jane's retreat in 1616. She had chosen detachment as the theme for her retreat, but at prayer found herself unable to concentrate because she was worried about Francis who was ill. In reply to her letter, Francis encouraged her on her path of detachment and her journey towards pure love. It was a sacrifice for both of them. It is important to recognise here that the initial impulse in this direction of detachment comes from Jane's own heart. Respectful of what God is calling her to, and listening to the voice of God in her desire, Francis confirms this movement of detachment. She is to give into God's safe-keeping all her concerns, including her relationship with him. In this way, Francis not only helped her to respond to her deepest desire, but also ensured that autonomy and sense of self that was beginning to flourish. However, it was not without a cost for both of them, and Jane, in writing about this newfound freedom declares:

> Oh God, how easy it is to leave what is outside ourselves. But to leave one's skin, one's flesh, one's bones and penetrate into the deepest part of the marrow, which is, it seems to me, what we have done, is a great, difficult, and impossible thing to do except for the grace of God.[31]

The eventual outcome was a recognition that the God who had called them together was now asking them to re-focus their relationship, allowing Jane to grow in independence, so necessary for the governance of the order. This 'detachment' was an extremely painful process for both. However, the authenticity of their spiritual friendship can be gauged by the fruit it bore. Not only was it mutually enriching and transformative for Francis and Jane, but it was to ripen and produce fruit beyond itself – giving birth to the visitation sisters.

THE FOUNDATION OF THE VISITATION SISTERS:

Francis had not intended to found an order in the strict sense of the term, but a simple congregation. He didn't realise that the rigorous strictures that the Council of Trent had insisted upon for monastic life, would also effect his nascent congregation.[32] Thus, as the institute flourished he was pressurised into adopting the cloister. Originally, he had intended that the sisters would be 'congregated' to assist the poor and sick of Annecy. Indeed, he had at first thought of renouncing solemn vows and replacing them by 'the unique bond of love'.[33] Francis wanted the visitation sisters to be a community of friends, giving witness to this spiritual friendship, bonded by charity.

One of the original aspects of this congregation was that they opened their door to all those who 'because of their age or some physical weakness, cannot have access to more austere monasteries, provided they are healthy in mind and willing to live a life of humility, obedience, simplicity, gentleness and resignation'.[34] Their aim was to combine prayer and service to the poor and the sick. For this reason they chose Our Lady of the Visitation as their patron:

> The image of the visitation of the Virgin Mary was more than a pious insignia for the envisioned congregation. It was expressive of both the structure and the inner meaning of the life the two friends intended to initiate. For them, love of God and love of neighbour together represented the fullest response of the individual to the call from God. In the image of the Visitation the two were exquisitely expressed.[35]

In this way, those who were admitted to the congregation and those to whom they ministered, were among 'the little ones'. This was to be a visible sign of God's love. This confidence in the love of God is to be the kernel of their life, and is constantly repeated by Francis to them in his *Conferences*:

> You wish further to know the foundation our confidence ought to have. It must be grounded on the infinite goodness of God and on the merits of the death and the passion of our Lord Jesus Christ, with this condition on our part, that we should preserve and recognise in ourselves an entire and firm resolution to belong wholly to God and to abandon ourselves in all things and without any reserve to his providence.[36]

Certain of the love of God for them, Jane and Francis give expression to this certainty through the birth of the congregation.

Eternal Friendship:

> The friendship that can end was never true friendship ...
> Friendship based on the world passes away but our friendship which is from God, in God and for God, never ends.[37]

A spiritual friendship 'never changes except into a more perfect union of spirits, a living image of the blessed friendship existing in heaven'.[38] So Francis sees the love of friendship as the beginning of the kind of happiness that we will experience in heaven where we will be a source of joy to one another. He says this explicitly in the meditation on Paradise in *The Introduction*:

> The blessed 'give to one another ineffable contentment and live in the consolation of a happy and indissoluble union'.[39]

Love remains forever, though the other charisms pass away (1 Cor 13:13). As the friends grow in closeness with God and one another, their friendship as symbol expresses ever more fully and perfectly the reality of God's own love working in the hearts of us all. The more our friendship is rooted in the Lord and expresses friendship with him, the broader our hearts are in loving a multitude of others. This is the ecstatic nature of true friendship. But if love for a friend gives us power to love others, then certainly it increases our power to love our friend.

Thus, friendship is meant to last forever. It is not a stage that falls away when we have used it to come to divine intimacy and to universal love of mankind. It is not a mere means to God which is to be cast aside when it has served its purpose. We do not love others only as a means to friendship with God. Persons are never a means to an end, but always to be loved for their own sake. A person is always an end in himself or herself. As an end in itself, of course, it is subordinate to the ultimate end. It is part of the fullness of the ultimate end, which is our communion with God in communion with all his friends. And as Francis says:

> Friendships begun in this world will be taken up again, never to be broken off ...[40]

Mary, Model for the Spiritual Life

Jesus manifests the depth of his love by embracing the will of the Father. This union of wills is perfectly imitated by Mary. She is the first to 'put on Christ' and through Christ has access to the Father:

> The Virgin Mary, redeemed in a more exalted fashion by reason of the merits of her Son, is endowed with the high office and dignity of the Mother of the Son of God … She occupies a place in the church which is the highest after Christ, and also closest to us.[1]

A heart that loves:

Francis understands fully the communion that exists between Mary and her son Jesus. There is a unity of hearts. 'Out of devotion to Our Lord is born immediately devotion to Our Lady. No one can love the one without loving the other.'[2] Often he will write about them as having one heart:

> Our house of the Visitation is noble enough to have its own coat of arms. I thought, my dear mother, if you agree to it, to choose as coat of arms a heart pierced with two arrows, surmounted by a cross and enclosed in a crown of thorns, the sacred names of Jesus and Mary being engraved upon it … for truly, our little congregation is the work of the heart of Jesus and Mary.[3]

However, he also emphasises her solidarity with us. His understanding of the role of Mary is identical with that of the Vatican Council. She is placed firmly in the heart of the church. There is no church without the Holy Spirit, without a bond of love. This Spirit is given only to those who want to come together with an open mind and join themselves to the Mother of Jesus.[4] Indeed, in his first sermon on the feast of Pentecost, he declares:

> If like the apostles and disciples we begin with one heart and mind to pray to God with devotion together with Mary the mother of Jesus, we will receive the Holy Spirit ... For no one can have Jesus Christ for a brother who will not have Mary for mother; and he who will not be a brother of Jesus Christ, will no longer be a co-heir.[5]

The prayer of Jesus that all may be one is given concrete expression in this ecclesial understanding that we must join ourselves with Mary, like the disciples, in order to receive the Holy Spirit, the source of unity. Mary is created to 'attract and lead all people to her Son'.[6] It is for this reason that Francis encourages 'honour, reverence, and respect for her ... just as young nightingales learn to sing in company with the old, so also by our holy association with (her) and the saints, let us learn the best way to pray and sing God's praise'.[7] However, Francis does add a note of caution when he writes:

> A person who desires to please God and Our Lady does what is very good, but one who would like to please Our Lady as much as God or more than God would commit an intolerable breach of order ... to each end we must give its proper rank, and consequently supreme rank to the end of pleasing God.[8]

The Way of Lowliness:
Mary, understood from a biblical and ecclesial perspective, has a unique place in the plan of God and much to teach us about our own spiritual journey. In a letter to Jane Frances de Chantal, he encourages her to meditate on the life of Mary so as to 'put on Christ':

> See your Abbess wherever she is. In her room at Nazareth, she exercises her simplicity in desiring to be taught and asking questions, her lowliness and humility in calling herself a handmaid. See her in Bethlehem: She leads a holy life of poverty, she listens to the shepherds as if they had been great doctors. Contemplate her in the company of the kings: She is

not busy in making speeches to them. See her at the Purification: she goes to the Temple in obedience to the ecclesiastical custom. Going to Egypt, and returning hence, she obeys St Joseph with simplicity. She does not think a waste of time in visiting her cousin Elizabeth, in charitable simplicity. She goes seeking Our Lord not rejoicing but weeping. She has compassion for the poverty and confusion of those who invited her for the wedding at Cana, humble, lowly and virtuous.[9]

A model of all the virtues, Mary excels above all in her love for God. Like Jesus, meek and humble of heart, Mary enters into the path of lowliness. It is the same path that Francis encourages his correspondents to take when he writes, 'Let us keep to our lower but safer way. It is less excellent but better suited to our lack and littleness. If we conduct ourselves with humility and good faith in this, God will raise us up to heights that are truly great.'[10]

Mary's recognition of her own lowliness and complete dependence on God, opens her up to receive abundantly from God's generosity. This is what she calls us to, but 'to receive God's grace into our hearts, they must be emptied of our own vainglory.[11] When she sings in her *Magnificat* 'that Our Lord has regarded the humility of his handmaid, all generations shall call her blessed, she means that our Lord has graciously looked down on her lowliness in order to heap graces and favours upon her.'[12] It is this emptiness of heart that attracts the gaze of God.

What Mary recognises is a fundamental truth of human nature – that we are dependent on God who has created us. Francis names this as the state of humility. He then proceeds to demonstrate how Mary accepts this state which leads her then to exercise the virtue of humility. The humility that Mary exhibits is aligned to truth for she recognises her own nothingness and emptiness, but she also recognises God's generosity and desire to fill that nothingness and emptiness. It is a false humility, therefore, to not recognise what we have received from God as his gift. Francis encourages us as follows:

Let us consider what he has done for us ...There is no need to

fear that knowledge of his gifts will make us proud if only we
remember this truth, that none of the good in us comes from
ourselves ... What good do we possess that we have not received? And if we have received it, why do we glory in it? ...
Thus, the Blessed Virgin proclaims that God has done great
things for her, but she does only to humble herself and to
glorify God. 'My soul magnifies the Lord, because he has
done great things for me', she says.[13]

True humility, as lived by Mary, recognises that all is gift. There
is a real correlation between humility and charity. Francis proceeds to ask, how can something so high as charity and low as
humility come together, be united? He finds an answer in the
hidden mystery of the Visitation:

Does the Visitation of Our Lady to Elizabeth not seem to rep-
resent this union of humility and charity? Are these two
virtues not practiced by Our Lady towards her cousin?
Humility and charity have only one object which is God –
nonetheless, they pass from God to one's neighbour and it is
there where they are perfected.[14]

In this mystery as lived by Mary, Francis sees the call of every
Christian to 'clasp God to our heart' and 'carry him in our
arms'.[15]

The path of childlike simplicity
It is trust and confidence in God, which Mary lives supremely,
that is the hallmark of an authentic spirituality. It is the call to
become a child and trust in God our Father, as Francis writes:

We are related to God by such close alliance and such loving
dependence that nothing prevents us from saying that he is
our Father and from calling us his children.[16]

Nowhere in the teaching of Jesus are we given a technique to follow.[17] Instead, Jesus praises the poor in spirit. He encourages a
childlike attitude towards God our Father and openness to receive in faith. What is required is a childlike simplicity that can
speak the 'yes'. This is Mary's childlike response to the angel

when she says, 'Let what you have said be done to me' (Lk 1:38). In this manner she lives the maxim 'ask for nothing, refuse nothing'. She is open to receive what God desires to give, his love. It is this attitude that Francis seeks to inculcate in his correspondents so that they may learn to use or sacrifice all created things in the interest of love.

What is required is true emptiness which is to be found in the *anawim* to which Mary belongs. A complete and utter dependence on God. An emptiness of heart that allows God to shower it with his abundance. Mary, and those who imitate her emptiness, put up no barrier to the generosity of God who loves to give. Poor in spirit, she offers an empty space which can be inhabited by God.

This state of childhood simplicity is not a transitional phase in our spiritual development. The incarnation reveals to us the eternal meaning of being born. We are always beginners. It is God who takes the initiative and invites us to follow. To become a true disciple of Christ, like Mary, is to allow ourselves to be led by God. As a woman of prayer Mary exhibits this desire to be led by God, to do his will. In the dialogue of 'heart speaking to heart' Mary ponders the word of God, an attitude that Francis recommends we imitate:

> Be devoted to the word of God whether you hear it in familiar conversation with spiritual friends or in sermons ... Do all this after the example of the most holy Virgin, for she carefully kept in her heart all the words spoken in praise of her child.[18]

This conversation with God is made possible because God is first to speak. Once again, in this dialogue, we are always beginners. We can never reach a stage where we assume control. It is God who always takes the initiative.

This acknowledgement of childlike simplicity is manifested in the ability to wait on God. Mary is a perpetual advent, 'the morning star which brings us gracious news of the advent of the true Sun'.[19] The virtue exhibited in waiting is one of 'holy indifference'.[20] By this, Francis does not mean apathy, rather a single-mindedness where our only concern is to please God.

Indifference is only made possible by love and 'there is no one except the most holy Virgin Our Lady who has perfectly attained to this degree of excellence in love for her dearly beloved'.[21] It is a complete trust in God and surrender to God's will.

> The indifferent heart is like a ball of wax in God's hands, ready to receive all the impressions of his eternal good pleasure. It is a heart without choice, equally ready for all things and having no other object for its will except the will of God.[22]

Initially, this may appear unpleasant, even harsh, but Francis assures us that this complete trust and confidence in God serves as a counter-weight to the various changes brought about by the conditions of life. If our heart is not fixed on God. then tribulations from without in the circumstances of life and tribulations from within will leave us feeling at sea. And so, he writes:

> You should look from time to time at God, like mariners who to arrive at the port they are bound for look at the sky above them rather than down on the sea on which they sail. Thus God will work with you, in you, and for you, and after your labour consolation will follow.[23]

In speaking of Mary's discipleship, Francis stresses that although her heart was centred on God, this did not mean that she was spared suffering.[24] Indeed, the opposite is true, because she shares fully in the suffering of her Son out of love:

> Her Son's sorrow at that time was a piercing sword that passed through the mother's heart, for that mother's heart was fastened, joined, and united to her son in so perfect a union that nothing could wound the one without inflicting the keenest torture upon the other.[25]

In union with Jesus, she enters fully into the mystery of his death and resurrection. She is at one with this movement of love that issues from the heart of God. Through her obedience in love, 'there was no longer a union but rather a unity of heart, soul and life between this mother and this son … If this mother lived her son's life, she also died her son's death'.[26] While it is true that Mary is privileged by God, she knows only too well our human struggles, as 'she had part in all human miseries'.[27] She encourages us amidst trials to turn our focus on God:

No matter what course the ship may take, no matter whether it sails to the east, west, north, or south, no matter what wind drives it on, the mariner's needle never points in any direction except toward the fair polar star. Everything may be in confusion not only around us, I say, but within us as well. Our soul may be overwhelmed with sorrow or joy, with sweetness or bitterness, with peace or trouble ... for all that ever and always our heart's point, our spirit, our higher will, which is our compass, must unceasingly look and tend toward the love of God, its Creator, its Saviour, its sole sovereign good.[28]

Mary participates in our human struggle. She knows what it is to lose Jesus as we see her searching in the Temple. When she does find him she doesn't understand his reply, but 'ponders these things in her heart'(Lk 2:51). She will realise the full significance of his words when she stands at the foot of the cross, 'do you not know that I must be about my Father's business?'(Lk 2:49). She is familiar with loss and grief. She knows what it's like to be afraid when God intervenes in her life with his plan. At the annunciation she could easily have gone down the route of anxiety, asking countless questions, wondering how things would turn out, would Joseph and others understand? Would they believe her? Interestingly enough, the angel is aware of her fear and doesn't allow her to dwell on it. Rather he points out that God will bring this about, all she has to do is to let it happen to her. Mary is perturbed, but it is not her feelings that dictate her response. Her response issues from the depths of her heart in faith and love, trusting when she doesn't understand.

Mary Our Mother and Guide

She is our own mother in an especial way. Let us run to her and like little children cast ourselves into her arms with perfect confidence. At every moment and on every occasion let us call on this dear mother. Let us invoke her maternal love and by trying to imitate her virtues let us have true filial affection for her.[29]

Francis believes that there is a mutual affection between Mary and us, that she mothers us into Christ. Her own mystery of receiving and carrying Christ is our own deepest mystery. It is not simply a possibility, but a reality. We have noted how the incarnation is not simply an historical reality, but also a continuous metaphysical and personal fact. No longer servants, we are formed anew as his friends. Therefore, Christ is not simply an exterior model to be imitated, but imprints his mystery in our heart. And so, the image of God within us takes on a christological dimension. Through the incarnation our natural being is re-clothed with the beauty of the Son who becomes the 'window' through which the Father gazes on us. Although this is our deepest reality, it is a hidden reality of which, often, we are totally unaware. And yet, 'the artist is not ignorant of his art, even though we are ignorant of it'.[30]

As mother, Mary co-operates with the salvific plan of God, desiring to awaken us to this fundamental truth, to live Jesus as she did:

> Paul no longer lived himself but Jesus Christ lived in him because of that most close union of his heart with his Master's whereby his soul were as if dead in the heart it animated so as to live in the Saviour's heart which it loved ... how much truer is it that the sacred Virgin and her Son had but one soul, but one heart and one life, so that the Blessed Mother, although living yet did not live herself but rather her Son lived in her![31]

Francis is at pains to help us understand that God made Mary 'pass through all states of life, so that all people may find in her whatever they need to live well in their own state of life'.[32] In her we see what is possible whenever there is openness to God, trust, confidence and surrender. Surrender, the way of love, is not the way of achievement, but the way of fruitfulness. Mary is our model in this regard. By emptying herself, she receives the fullness of God. By being open, God is able to do great things in her. She is fruitful.

In imitation of Mary, Francis counsels us to 'offer him your heart so that he may make himself its sole master.[33] ... As our beloved Jesus lives in your heart, so too he will live in all your conduct ... With St Paul you can say these holy words, "It is no longer I that live, but Christ lives in me".'[34] This is the core of living a gospel spirituality as outlined by St Francis de Sales. It is to enter into this reality of imitating Jesus so that his mystery may grow within us and become a concrete reality in our daily lives, so that he may walk again in our world today. Such a reality will undoubtedly face us with the cross where we enter into the Paschal rhythm of the Christian life, a passage from death to life in Christ:

> Within your soul you have Jesus Christ, the most precious child in the world, and until he is entirely brought forth and born you cannot help suffering from your labour. But be of good heart ... He will be wholly brought forth for you when you have wholly formed him in your heart and deeds by imitating his life.[35]

Mary entered into this mystery through her yes to God and invites us to co-operate with God in our restoration. Above all she invites us to open ourselves to the love of God knowing that 'on the tree of the cross the heart of Jesus, our beloved, beheld (our) heart and loved it'.[36] He loves us in such a way as if we were the only one. He calls our prodigal heart back to its true home. God knows that our heart 'will not find a place of rest, any more than did the dove that went out from Noah's ark, so that it may return to himself from whom it came'.[37] We see fulfilled in Mary the true destiny of our heart which is the paradise of God, the dwelling place of God.

> May Our Lord bless your heart and set it afire with love of him! May he alone be your heart's delight; may your sole comfort be the seeking of his glory in all you do. May he make his home in your heart and may you find your refuge in his.[38]

Notes

CHAPTER ONE

1. For a well documented presentation of the predestination crisis cf. the Introduction written by André Ravier, *Oeuvres*, Paris, Editions Gallimard, 1969, xxviii-xxxiii. For our presentation on the crisis we are indebted to the scholarly work of E.M. Lajeunie, *Saint François de Sales: The Man, The Thinker, His Influence*, Tr. 2 vols. Rory O' Sullivan, Bangalore, SFS Publications, 1987. (This book, with appropriate volume, will be cited hereafter as, Lajeunie). We will follow his outline in differentiating the different stages of the crisis spanning his student days at Paris and Padua.
2. For a detailed study of his early student days cf. Elizabeth Stopp 'Francis de Sales at Clermont College' in *Salesian Studies* (Winter 1969) 42-63.
3. Francis Ronis, friend of St Francis de Sales, gives this account at the Process for Beatification – Processus t.III, p.9.
4. Lajeunie, vol. I, 66
5. Premier Proces Remissiorial d'Annecy, 4 – all these texts can be read at length with a description of the trial in *Oeuvres* XXII, pp12-22.
6. Henri Bremond has a beautiful commentary on this drama and suggests that it was similar to the dark night experienced by Pascal. He suggests that it originated from a current theology of despair and that it was chiefly a question of dogma, 'a particular school of theology had either caused or intensified it'. Bremond refers to the Thomist school. When the crisis passed as Francis dedicated his life to the mercy of God at the foot of the black Virgin, Bremond says, 'It is as if a leprous scale fell away, and with it the system that had caused it.' Henri Bremond, *Histoire Littéraire du Sentiment religieux en France, depuis la fin des guerres de religion jusqu'à nos jours. Tome I: L'humanisme dévote* (1580-1660), Paris, Ed. A. Colin, 1967, pp. 88-91.
7. Pierre Serouet, François de Sales, in *Dictionnaire de Spiritualité* ,Tome V, Paris, Beauchesne, 1964, 1078.
8. A. Liuima, *Aux Sources du Traité de l'amour de Dieu de Saint François de Sales*, 2 Vols, Libraire Editrice de L'université Gregorienne, 1960. (Hereafter: Liuima)
9. cf. Lajeunie Vol. I, 85-86. The kind of determinist opinion that Francis came up against at Padua which he found 'tougher than iron' and which he thought belonged to St Thomas, was really an error created by the inept translation of Henri de Ghent (1220-95).

Thus, the position he rejects is not that of St Thomas but of one of his interpreters. He had translated 'quos reprobat' as meaning that for God to reprove was for God to want men to sin so that he could punish them and thus demonstrate the glory of his justice.

10. cf. *Oeuvres* XXII,64-64. It is clear that he had decided to take leave of their opinion, but in these pages we can see the anguish it caused him.

11. *Oeuvres* XXII, 64-64.

12. cf. Alexander Pocetto, 'An Introduction to Salesian Anthropology' in *Salesian Studies*, 6 (Summer, 1969) 32-62.

13. Bremond and Vincent argue that the studies undergone by Francis were Thomistic. However, there are two manuscripts dated 15 Dec 1590 in *Oeuvres*: XII, 46-47; 51-63 that would indicate that under the guidance of the Jesuits Francis followed the theme of 'post praevisa merita et demerita'. cf. Louis Cognet, *Histoire de la Spiritualité Chrétienne*, Paris, Editions Aubier-Montaigne, 1966, 290. Cognet, among others, accepts that Francis found a resolution to the crisis of despair through Molinist's ideas on grace and predestination. Molinism advocates the priority of freedom of the human will, that is, God does not predestine people either to heaven or hell. Whatever occurs in the future is determined by human free choice. God is not the cause of the choice nor does God predetermine any particular choices made. Nevertheless, he does foresee the future as it will occur. Francis takes comfort in such understanding of freedom and predestination, but in other areas does not hold the Molinist School of thought.

14. Liuima, Vol. I, 27

15. *Oeuvres* V:296.

16. *Oeuvres* IV:228. cf. also IV:85; IV:136; V:169.

17. T. Tyrell, *Urgent Longings*, Massachusetts, Affirmation Books, 1980, 19. For a comprehensive treatment of this theme cf. *John of the Cross: Collected Works*, trans. Kieran Kavanaugh & Otilio Rodriguez, Washington D.C., Institute of Carmelite Studies Publications, 1973, 377-649.

18. *Oeuvres* III:261.

19. *Oeuvres* XXII, 19-20. Apart from this prayer there is practically no first hand account written by Francis as regards what he endured. The evidence rests on his servants, tutor Déage and two fellow-students. We also have Francis's own account to St Jane de Chantal, as well as some written evidence preserved through the letters in which Francis had expressed his feelings, but the whole correspondence of the Paris years was burnt when the castle at Thorens was looted and burnt in 1634.

20. As he himself says, 'pure love is a love "with which God is loved for himself and by which the whole heart is given to him" the whole heart without any reservation.' *Oeuvres* VII,397. And this pure love,

which exactly defines our relation to God, is to be found in Mary who is its living paradigm. cf. Book 9, ch. 11-16 *Treatise*, to explore in detail this 'death to self' which takes place in the will and moves on the path to pure love.

21. *Lajeunie* Vol. I, 109
22. *Lajeunie* Vol. I, 72

CHAPTER TWO

1. Henri Bremond writes, 'How can I not cite here the chapters of higher philosophy which open the *Treatise* on the Love of God, and compare them line for line with the parallel chapters of Calvin on the misery of man.' The human person is not left without resources, even as regards nature, and if, in order to raise to God, God himself is necessary, he does not hesitate to add very correctly that the effort of man himself is necessary and this effort is neither impossible nor in vain.

2. It is interesting to note again how Francis's understanding of the human person reveals something about the nature of God. It is in understanding ourselves that we come to appreciate the God who has created us. The God who 'gently holds us' and 'draws us to himself'. We allow ourselves to be held and drawn by God when we respond to this natural inclination within us, which is to go in search of love.

3. *Oeuvres* IV:74.
4. C. F. Kelley, *Spirit of Love*, New York, Harper, 1951, 47.
5. *Oeuvres* IV:74-75.
6. *Oeuvres* V:165.
7. The Salesian understanding of the human person is marked by the neo-stoicism of the sixteenth century. The neo-stoics' aim was to marry the wisdom of the stoics with Christian teaching. In the original draft of book Five in the *Treatise*, when he's writing about how love employs the cardinal virtues, he uses the image of the four rivers of paradise. It is in this context that he describes the human heart as being the dwelling place, paradise of God.

8. *Oeuvres* V:268-269.
9. Francis quips that often we amuse ourselves by wondering if we are very good angels, when we would be better off trying to be good men and women. cf. *Oeuvres* XII, 204.
10. *Oeuvres* IV,192-193.
11. *Oeuvres* IV:40.
12. *Oeuvres* V:161.
13. *Oeuvres* IV:40
14. cf. Alexander Pocetto, *An Introduction to Salesian Anthropology*, p. 6.
15. André Ravier, *Ce Que Croyait François de Sales*, p. 7.

16. Francis makes use of two expressions in the *Treatise* to capture this reality: *fond du coeur* (six times) *Oeuvres* IV:78; IV:154; IV:306; IV:327; V:329; V:337; and *milieu du coeur* (eleven times) *Oeuvres* IV:179; IV:269; IV:329; V:42; V:78; V:79; V:154; V:259; V:324. Both expressions deal with our relationship with God. They speak not of an activity, but rather, of a state of being, a passivity in which we experience the indwelling of the Trinity. It is the place where Jesus is present as a captain in the centre of a fortress and gives us help in the moment of temptation. cf. Book III, ch. 3.

17. *Oeuvres* IV:67.

18. *The Devout Life,* Book II, ch. 12-13.

19. According to Francis, the rational soul has three courts: that which reasons according to sense knowledge, that which reasons according to purely human knowledge, and that which draws its conclusions from the data of revelation. But beyond these areas is the supreme point of the soul, the centre of our personality. cf. Alexander Pocetto, *An Introduction to Salesian Anthropology.* For a comprehensive treatment of this theme cf. T. Poli, *Punta Suprema dell'Anima,* Rome, Università Gregoriana Editrice, 1982, 43-73.

20. *Oeuvres* V:309

21. André Ravier, *Un Sage et Un Saint: François de Sales,* Paris, Nouvelle Cité, 1985, 128.

22. *Oeuvres* IV:197

23. *Oeuvres* IV:90

24. cf. *Oeuvres* IV:136; IV:187; IV:256

25. This idea is certainly not unique to Francis, it is expounded by Augustine (the restless heart) among others. It's a theme which is to be found in modern theology, cf. Lonergan's ideas of 'transcendent love', i.e. an inherent desire for truth, beauty, and absolute kindness, a desire which surpasses all terrestrial objects. According to Lonergan, this desire is a given of our anthropological basis, perhaps temporarily eclipsed by less elevated and passionate needs, but which hides in an indestructible fashion in the depths of the human heart.

26. *Oeuvres* IV:78-79.

27. *Oeuvres* IV:78.

28. *Oeuvres* V:144.

29. *Oeuvres* XV:89

30. This idea is not original to Francis. It can be seen clearly in Pauline writings, the struggle between the old man and the new man – Adam and Christ – two men, one rebellious toward God and the other obedient. cf. *Oeuvres* VII:6.

31. *Oeuvres* XVI:241-243, W. Wright and J. Power, *Letters of Spiritual Direction,* New York, Paulist Press, 1988, 164-165.

32. We are imperfect and yet we have a desire for perfection. Since we cannot find satisfaction within we go beyond ourselves to be lost in

another. This ecstasy, this moving out of self, can lead to either a lowering of oneself by getting lost in sensuality or an elevating of oneself towards the divinity. Even modern spirituality speaks of this:

'... as people of flesh we are easily seduced to a downward transcendence of emotionalism, sensualism, disquietude, discouragement, fear and lust. This downward transcendence, although it represents a search for communion, takes us in a direction that carries us away from the possibility of real communion, in the manner of a false light. More intense loneliness is the inevitable result.' (Thomas Merton, *New Seeds of Contemplation*, New York, New Directions Books, 1972, 90-97). This distinction between 'downward transcendence' and a transcendence that leads to 'real communion' is akin to the two ecstasies described by St Francis de Sales: sensual pleasure and spiritual delights. An understanding of these two ecstasies are essential if we are to appreciate the dynamics of love and its tragedies in the *Treatise*.

33. cf. His commentary on St Paul, *Oeuvres* VII:6
34. *Oeuvres* IV:94.
35. cf. Book I,16 in the *Treatise*
36. cf. Book X,12. To understand Francis here, a distinction must be made between the 'already' and the 'not yet' of our resemblance to God. The 'already' is our possession of the love dimension of the divine resemblance. The 'not yet' is the imperative to actualise or realise the resemblance by loving as God loves. We have a potential to love but are free; therefore, we may love selflessly and realise the divine image in us or we may choose not to. Louis Lavelle commenting on this states: 'Whoever complains that he/she cannot love remains on the surface of self and allows the spectacle of the world either to distract him or imprison him in the cavern of self; thus we will know nothing of the infinity of love, save a few impulses immediately checked by self-love.' (Louis Lavelle, *Quatre Saints: Saint François de Sales*, 194).
37. Book I, 17 *Treatise*.
38. Book 2,16 *Treatise*.
39. *ibid*.
40. Book I, 18 *Treatise*.

CHAPTER THREE

1. It is in the *Treatise* itself that Francis reveals how he has been introduced to the *Song of Songs* through the scholarly work of Gilbert Genebrard, cf. *Oeuvres* V:277. This commentary by Genebrard was published in 1585 and contains in essence the contents of the course Francis took. Indeed, Francis was to write his own commentary on the *Song of Songs*. The text with a commentary, translated into English, can be read in full: A. Brix, *St François de Sales and the Canticle of Canticles*, Bangalore, SFS Publications, 1989.

2. For a fuller understanding of this relationship between creation and the incarnation, cf. *Oeuvres* IV:102-105.
3. *Oeuvres* IV:196-197.
4 *Oeuvres* IV:91. The original French text captures much more clearly this sense of creation as being a present, continuous action of love: *'Cette perfection est un seul acte ... lequel n'estant autre chose que la propre essence divine.'* Note the use of *estant* to express God's nature as being act (cf. also *Oeuvres* V:210 *estant le souverain bien*). This use of the present continuous is reminiscent of the Hebraic notion of being *(eyheh)* which, more than indicating a state of being, indicates an activity, being present with. For Francis, the being of God expresses a continual movement, creating and speaking ceaselessly through creation.
5. *Oeuvres* V:343.
6. *Oeuvres* IV:91.
7. *Oeuvres* IV:87
8. *Oeuvres* IV:96-97
9. *Oeuvres* V:343.
10. *Oeuvres* IV:243
11. *Oeuvres* V:110-111
12. *Oeuvres* V:113
13. *Oeuvres* IV:99
14. R. Bady, *François de Sales*, Paris, Desclée De Brouwer,1970, p. 27.
15. *St Francis de Sales: Selected Letters*, Trans. Elizabeth Stopp, London, Faber & Faber, 1960, 261. cf also *Oeuvres* IV:243
16. *Oeuvres* IV:99-102
17. Lajeunie, Vol. I:168.
18. cf. *Oeuvres* IV:99
19. *Oeuvres* X:166
20. cf. *Oeuvres* 198-199
21. *Oeuvres* IV:136
22. cf. *Oeuvres* V:208-213
23. *Oeuvres* V:210
24 cf. *Oeuvres* V:188-191. This ecstasy in God is prompted by a quality which Francis describes as kindness *(bonté)*, which expresses God's total gift of self, an outgoing in kindness which holds nothing back for itself. Hèlene Bordes sees an intimate connection between this *bonté* of God and God's desire to communicate. cf. H. Bordes 'François de Sales et la Béatitude des Miséricordieux' in *La Vie Spirituelle* 146 (Mars-Avril 1992) 177-189.
25. cf. *Oeuvres* IV:40
26. Francis explicitly acknowledges St Dionysisus the Pseudo-Areopagite as the source of this understanding of God as ecstatic love. God's ecstasy, the deity's standing outside itself, is an excess of goodness that overflows in a loving and creative procession down to humanity. At the basis of such an understanding is the

Neoplatonic metaphysics of 'procession and return', that is, all reality proceeds from God and is gathered back to its divine source. For further understanding of the Salesian understanding of ecstatic love, cf. *Oeuvres* V:24.

27. *Oeuvres* V:230.
28. *Oeuvres* IV:275.
29. cf. *Oeuvres* IV:84.
30. cf.*Oeuvres* IV:99-102.
31. *Oeuvres* IV:100.
32. A. Ravier, *Ce Que Croyait François de Sales*, Paris, Mame, 1976, 75.
33. cf.*Oeuvres* IV:109.
34. For a fuller understanding of this relationship between creation and incarnation, cf. *Oeuvres* IV:102-105.
35. cf. *Oeuvres* IV:103.
36. Brix, 25-26.
37. *Oeuvres* IV:103.
38. Lajeunie, Vol. II, 395.
39. L. S. Fiorelli, 'The Holy Spirit in the Thought of St Francis of Sales' in *Salesianum* 52 (1990), 325.
40. *Oeuvres* IV:100.
41. L. S. Fiorelli, 'The Holy Spirit in the Thought of St Francis of Sales' in *Salesianum* 52 (1990), 325.
42. *Oeuvres* X:413.
43. This idea is developed in Bk. II, Ch. 4 and Ch. 5.
44. Mueller, 30.
45. *Oeuvres* IV:104.
46. *Oeuvres* X:273
47. *Oeuvres* IV:104.
48. Kelley, 59.
49. *Oeuvres* V:11.
50. *Oeuvres* IV:84.
51. *Oeuvres* IV:104.
52. cf. Bk. V, ch. 2; ch. 5.
53. *Oeuvres* IV:260.
54. *Oeuvres* V:29.
55. E. M. Lajeunie, *St François de Sales et l'ésprit Salésien*, Paris, Editions du Seuil, 1962, 119.
56. Lajeunie, Vol. II, 583.
57. The witness of meekness and humility are inseparable and both depend on charity. Francis describes humility as 'a descending charity' and meekness as the 'flower of charity'. *Oeuvres* III:162.
58. *Oeuvres* V:230.
59. *Oeuvres* V:230.
60. *Oeuvres* VI:62-63.
61. The French word *abaissement*, as used by Francis to express Jesus

humbling himself, captures more vividly this sense of downward movement, of Jesus lowering himself.

62. *Oeuvres* IV:117.
63. *Oeuvres* IV:112. This idea that God desires us to be his pervades the *Treatise*, but is to be explicitly found in *Oeuvres* IV:186-187;V:32-33.
64. This Johannine quotation is cited twice in Book 10 chapter 12 of the *Treatise*. The French text expresses more richly the idea of the ecstatic love that is present in Jesus' incarnation. In the strict etymological sense of the word ecstasy means a going out of oneself. This idea is well conveyed through the verbs *oter* and *quitter* which not only express his free choice to lay down his life but also express this sense of movement wherein he 'leaves himself', 'goes out of himself' (*je quitter moy mesme*).
65. *Oeuvres* IV:114
66. *Oeuvres* IV:101-102
67. *Oeuvres* V:161.
68. Francis refers to Plato who depicts love as 'poor and naked' (*Oeuvres* IV:356) and also to the phrase in the *Song of Songs*, 'stronger than death is love', and he further remarks that 'as death drags the soul from all things with a strong hand so love separates the soul from all other inclinations and purifies it from all admixture' (*Oeuvres* V:211). It is both poor and naked because 'it gives up everything for the loved object' (*Oeuvres* IV:356).
69. *Oeuvres* V:160
70. *Oeuvres* V:123-124.
71. *Oeuvres* V:148.
72. *Oeuvres* V:339-340
73. *Oeuvres* V:148.
74. *Oeuvres* III:359
75. *Oeuvres* IV:185.
76. *Oeuvres* IV:287.
77. *Oeuvres* IV:294
78. The Salesian understanding of beauty invokes a special type of seeing, not with the physical faculty of the sight, but rather a spiritual sense, an interior seeing. The biblical insight of understanding things at the level of *sarx* or at the level of *pneuma* captures this idea well. To see beauty involves the Greek notion of *theoria*, that is, contemplation. True beauty is not a surface reality but needs to be penetrated with the eyes of the heart. When we speak about beauty from a Salesian perspective, it is in the first place an experience (seeing) more than an aesthetic doctrine as in Plato, Hegel or Kant. It is a question of relationship which is only made possible by a dialogue between two beings who, in love, have access to beauty. There is no personal beauty nor participation in the divine beauty without this dialogue of which God takes the initiative. It is God who permits us to see his beauty through contemplation, which is why contempla-

tion is opposed to curiosity: 'In striving to raise our reasonings too high in divine things by curiosity, we grow vain or empty in our thoughts and instead of arriving at the knowledge of truth, we fall into the folly of our vanity' (*Oeuvres* IV:236). Curiosity is only interested in the exterior aspects of things; it does not go in search of understanding, only of seeing. It has nothing to do with observation and wonderment. Thus, to discover God's beauty and love involves a special type of seeing which is born from a faith relationship.

79. J. Sauté, *Jésus Christ dans l'histoire d'Amour de Dieu avec l'homme selon le 'Traité de l'amour de Dieu' de Saint François de Sales*, Memoire de Licence (typed, Bruxelles, Faculté de Théologie, 1991, 152)

80. *Oeuvres* IV:294-295

81. *Oeuvres* IV:102.

82. A. Ravier, *Ce Que Croyait François de Sales*, Paris, Labat, 1976, 111.

83. *Oeuvres* IV:99.

CHAPTER FOUR

1. cf. *Oeuvres* IV:51-52; IV:188-189; V:293.

2. *Oeuvres* V:293.

3. *Oeuvres* IV:163-164.

4. *Oeuvres* V:64.

5. *Oeuvres* IV:340.

6. *Oeuvres* IV:136.

7. The use of olfactive imagery is commonplace in oriental poetry, and prevalent in the *Song of Songs*. The image of God as perfume is evocative of his infinite goodness, beauty, sweetness, but above all, of his love, ie. of his desire to give of himself, to pour himself forth. When talking about being drawn by God's perfumes (*Oeuvres* IV:132;IV:162;V:15) it is more than probable that Francis is not simply referring to the physical sense of smell which attracts us, but also to the spiritual sense of smell. Within the tradition of the Fathers of the Church, it has been acknowledged that there are spiritual senses which correspond to the physical senses.

8. *Oeuvres* IV:132. The idea of God 'drawing' us is prevalent in the *Song of Songs*. In Hebrew, it is *mashakh*, a term belonging to a specifically prophetic vocabulary. For the prophets, it is one of the essential words of conversion. Thus we read in Jeremiah, 'I have loved you with an everlasting love, and this is why I draw you with kindness' (Jer 31:3).

9. .*Oeuvres* IV:133.

10. *Oeuvres* IV:234.

11. cf. Book II, ch. 9, ch. 12.

12. *Oeuvres* IV:115.

13. *Oeuvres* IV:129.

14. *Oeuvres* IV:128.

15. *Oeuvres* IV:116.

16. *Oeuvres* III:108-109.
17. *Oeuvres* IV:126-127.
18. *Oeuvres* IV:122.
19. *Oeuvres* IV:116.
20. *Oeuvres* IV:100.
21. *Oeuvres* IV:163-164. cf. also IV:295; IV:319; IV:331; V:19; V:196. In this regard, Francis is very Teresian in his understanding of prayer as friendship with Christ: 'Prayer in my opinion is nothing but an intimate conversation between friends; it means conversing frequently and alone with him who we know loves us.' (*Life*, 8,5).
22. *Oeuvres* IV:208.
23. *Oeuvres* IV:204.
24. *Oeuvres* IV:59.
25. *Oeuvres* IV:129.
26. *Oeuvres* III:74.
27. *Oeuvres* IV:260.
28. *Oeuvres* IV:273.
29. *Oeuvres* IV:345.
30. *Oeuvres* V:50-51.
31. *Oeuvres* XII:321.
32. cf. *Oeuvres* IV:337.
33 *Oeuvres* V:346.
34. *Oeuvres* III:261.
35. It is important to remember that contemplation is a gift; rather than something we do, it is what the Lord does to us. Contemplation is not a permanent state. The visitation of God is followed by withdrawal, an experience of absence. The benefit of this withdrawal is threefold. First, it prevents us from being 'puffed up'; second, God withdraws so that he may be desired more; third, we realise we do not have here our eternal home.
36. *Oeuvres* IV:340.
37. *Oeuvres* IV:52.
38. *Oeuvres* IV:310.
39. *Oeuvres* IV:324.
40. *Oeuvres* IV:332-333.
41. *Oeuvres* III:340.
42. *Oeuvres* IV:312.
43. *Oeuvres* III:92.
44. *Oeuvres* III:80.
45. In her *Way of Perfection* from chapters 4-15, Teresa names three virtues as essential as a solid basis for a life of prayer: love of neighbour, detachment, and humility. Up until this point, St Teresa says she has just been setting the board as you would do for a game of chess, because 'if we don't know how to set out the pieces we will never be able to play properly'. So 'setting the board' is living in a right way and she then proceeds to describe prayer in more detail.

We need Christ to train us, according to Teresa, in the theological and cardinal virtues. If we do not strive after these virtues we will always be 'dwarfs' (*Interior Castle* 7, 4, 9).
46. *Oeuvres* XIII:92.

CHAPTER FIVE

1. This is a rather unfortunate title because it suggests a polemic tone. This title was given to the writings by the publishers of the first edition, but Francis preferred to speak of them as meditations.
2. Adrienne Fichet, Premier Proces Remissorial d'Annecy, 32.
3. St Francis de Sales' commentary on Daniel 2:31-45.
4. Premier Proces Remissorial de Paris, 29.
5. Angelique Hullier, Premier Proces Remissorial de Paris, 32.
6. Fr Simon, Premier Proces Remissorial de Paris, 32.
7. Lajeunie Vol. II, 126.
8. Lajeunie. Vol. II, 113.
9. *Oeuvres* III:9
10. St Francis de Sales, *Thy Will Be Done: letters to Persons in the World*, New Hampshire, Sophia Press, 1995. It is suggested that *suavité* is a quality of gentleness in temperament; *douceur* is a quality of gentleness that is discovered through our senses. When Francis uses *sweet* it is a form of gentleness which sounds a bit strange to our ears. But gentleness is not to be equated with sentimentality; in fact, it is quite strong. Ryan in his introduction states: 'By such terms he wishes to describe all that is truly good and rightly cherished and held dear, all that is lovely, loving and lovable, all that is merciful, mild and kind, all that is most gentle even when most firm, all that checks and disciplines only to cleanse, strengthen and save, all that wishes only our good and seeks only to help us and to bring us to what we should be, all that is bright and joyous in itself and that alone can bring joy and peace to men's hearts.' cf. Mgr John D. Ryan's introduction to his translation, *Treatise on the Love of God* by St Francis de Sales, vol. 1, Rockford, Tan Books, 1975, 26.
11.   *Oeuvres* III:164.
12. *Oeuvres* III:165.
13. *Oeuvres* III:163-164.
14. *Oeuvres* III:165.
15. cf. *Oeuvres* III:166-168.
16. cf. the guidelines he gives the Visitation Sisters, especially conference 13 *Oeuvres* VI, as regards the particular spirit of their order.
17. *Oeuvres* X:342-342, Palm Sunday Sermon 20 March 1621.
18. cf. *Oeuvres* VI:71-73.
19. cf. *Oeuvres* VI, conference 70.
20. *Oeuvres* III, Third Part, section 5, Deeper interior humility.
21. *ibid.*
22. *ibid.*

23. St Francis de Sales, *Thy Will be Done: Letters to Persons in the World*, New Hampshire, Sophia Press, 1995, 135.
24. *Oeuvres* VI, conference 71.
25. *Oeuvres* III:154.
26. *Oeuvres* III:165.
27. *Oeuvres* III:166-167.
28. *Oeuvres* VI:76.
29. *Oeuvres* VI:67.
30. *Oeuvres* III:140.
31. *Oeuvres* V:230.
32. *Oeuvres* IV:99.
33. *Oeuvres* V:230.
34. *Oeuvres* V:230.
35. cf. Raniero Cantalamessa, *Life in the Lordship of Christ.*
36. Unfortunately, there does not appear to be any detailed study comparing the spirituality of St Francis de Sales and St Thérèse of Lisieux. We know that her aunt was a Visitation sister, her sister Leonie entered the Visitation monastery and her older sisters attended a Visitation school. In many ways her 'little way' is a concrete living out of the little virtues taught by St Francis de Sales.

CHAPTER SIX

1. *Oeuvres* VI, conference XII.
2. *Oeuvres* VI, conference XII.
3. *Oeuvres* VI, conference XII.
4. *Oeuvres* VI, conference XII.
5. *Oeuvres* VI:183-184.
6. The image of being 'carried' is one that goes beyond the boundaries of sexuality to indicate the loving tenderness of God. Hence, it refers to God as both father and mother. For example, cf. *Oeuvres* IV:126-127; IV:200; IV:243-244; IV:333; V:6; V:204.
7. *Oeuvres* V:313.
8. *Oeuvres* V:216-217.
9. *Oeuvres* V:216-217.
10. *Oeuvres* IV:201-202.
11. *Oeuvres* III:121.
12. *Oeuvres* XVIII:171. Letter to Sr Marie-Aimée de Blonay, 18 February 1618.
13. Above and beyond its historical context, the image of mother and father has a universal and perennial value. They are archetypal symbols 'which carry the same or very similar meanings for a large portion, if not all, of mankind' (P. Wheelwright, *Metaphor and reality*, 111). Through these symbols, Francis can be said to have constructed an ontological rather than a psychological approach to love. These symbols reveal that love is built into the nature of God and ourselves.

14. Henri Lemaire, *François de Sales: Docteur de la Confiance et de la Paix*, 27.

15. cf. Mueller, 64.

16. cf. the parable in Bk. 3, ch. 7, *Treatise*.

17. cf. *Oeuvres* III, 74-77.

18. cf. Henri Lemaire, *François de Sales: Docteur de la Confiance et de la Paix*, 177.

19. *Oeuvres* XIII:123, Letter to Jane de Chantal, 30 November 1605.

20. *Oeuvres* V:230.

21. *Oeuvres* V:301.

22. *Oeuvres* V:304-305, also V:293-294.

23. *Oeuvres* V:281.

24. *Oeuvres* XXIII:281-298, *Advertissemens aux confesseurs*.

25. *Oeuvres* XVIII:343, Letter to madame de Veyssilieu, 16 Jan. cf. also IV:126-127; IV:243-244; V:204.

26. cf. Mueller, 134. 'With Thomas Aquinas love stands in the background as the source and cause of holiness. In the foreground is the Lord of heaven and earth to whom we owe devotion and homage. With Francis this picture of Lord and servant is completely cut out in favour of the idea of the loving Father who awaits his child.'

27. *Oeuvres* V:152-153.

28. cf. *Oeuvres* IV:200; IV:333; V:6; V:10-11; V:69; V:191. Francis takes the line from the *Song of Songs* which originally was for the lover and beloved, 'kiss me with the kiss of your mouth' and translates this act of the spouse and the sulamite in a new way; it becomes the act of mother and child.

29. cf. Hos 11:8, God's womb is moved to compassion; cf. also Is 49:15; 66:12-13.

30. cf. Wright in *Bond of Perfection*, 60-61. 'There is a great tenderness in the way he takes the ordinary events of a woman's life and speaks to her of the spiritual dimensions which they can reveal.'

31. *Oeuvres* IV:192.

32. *Oeuvres* V:6.

33. *Oeuvres* IV:75-76.

34. H. Lemaire, *Les Image Chez St François de Sales*, Paris, Editions A.G. Nizet, 1962, 63.

35. *Oeuvres* V:69.

36. cf. P. Serouet, 'François de Sales' in *Dictionnaire de Spiritualité, tome v*, Paris, Beauchesne, 1964, 1088. 'Salesian Spirituality is centered on the abandon of the soul between the hands of God. Francis de Sales compares willingly this abandon to the attitude of a small child between the arms of its mother, an image which he'll borrow from the great castillian mystic. But Teresa of Avila does not develop the image; her love for the Lord was that of a spouse; she emphasises fidelity and intimacy; the summit of spiritual ascension is "marriage". We must ascribe to Francis to be situated in the long tradition of spiritual writers who before St Thérèse of Lisieux have presented

the relationship between the soul and God under the aspect of spiritual childhood.'

37. *Oeuvres* V:152-153 cf. also V:10.
38. This theme is analysed by Francis in Bk. 1 *Treatise,* cf. *Oeuvres* IV:23-85.
39. cf. H. Lemaire, *François de Sales: Docteur de la Confiance et de la Paix,* 27.
40. M. J. Buckley, 'Seventeenth Century French Spirituality: Three Figures' in L. Dupré and D. Saliers (ed.), *Christian Spirituality Post-Reformation and Modern,* SCM Press, 1989, 39.
41. cf. H. Lemaire, *François de Sales, Docteur de la Confiance et de la Paix,* 66.

CHAPTER SEVEN

1. *Oeuvres* VI:30.
2. Francis writes: 'Although the prodigal son returns naked, filthy, stinking, his fond father takes him into his arms, kisses him lovingly, weeps on his shoulder because he is his father and a father's heart feels for his child' *Oeuvres* XXIII:281-289. Why does the Father respond in such a way? Francis says quite simply that it is because he is his father. 'We belong to God' as the psalmist says – and 'a father is more tender-hearted than his children'.
3. *Oeuvres* IV:163-164.
4. *Oeuvres* VI:19.
5. *Oeuvres* XVIII:344.
6. *Oeuvres* IV:236.
7. *Letters to People in the World,* 99-100.
8. *Oeuvres* XIX:61.
9. Henri Lemaire, *François de Sales:Docteur de la Confiance et de la Paix,* 194. Thus, abandon is not simply to be equated with passivity. This is important, because Francis's teaching can be, and was, taken out of context to advocate a kind of lethargy, a passivity which is evident in Quietism. Jansenism reacted against this, and in turn created another heresy which emphasised personal sacrifice and mortification. Francis steers a middle course between these two heresies.
10. *Oeuvres* VI, conference 2.
11. As Kelley points out in *Spirit of Love,* 213, responding to this call of abandon, living a lifestyle in this manner, leads us to being born again because we annihilate ourselves 'not in nothing, but in that which is God. This explains why the virtue of holy indifference is not apathy or passivity; it may feel like it, but is far from fact.' In a word, this is to submit to the Spirit of God within.
12. *Oeuvres* III:171.
13. W. Wright & J. Power (eds) *Francis de Sales, Jane de Chantal: Letters of Spiritual Direction,* New York, Paulist Press, 1998, 67.
14. cf. love of submission, Book 9, *Oeuvres* V:109-163.
15. Why is abandon, surrender necessary? Because it is a condition and effect of love. The logic for Francis is this dialectic between abandonment and love. Without a progressive abandonment, love cannot

progress. Love increases indifference to all that which is not God. True love proceeds from God and is directed towards God. cf. H. Lemaire, *François de Sales: Docteur de la Confiance et de la Paix*, 176.

16. *Set Your Heart Free*, Indiana, Ave Maria Press, 1997, 143-145.

17. cf. *Oeuvres* V:169-170.

18. *Oeuvres* V:223.

19. *Set Your Heart Free*, Notre Dame, Ave Maria Press,1997, 143-145.

20. It is the same zeal of the lover in the *Canticle of Canticles* who will run the way of the beloved – the eager waiting is replaced by doing the will of God. This is well described by Francis in the *Treatise* in books 8 & 9. However, to avoid a distorted understanding of the books, it is necessary to ground them in the two preceding books, 6 & 7. Books 8 & 9 deal with our effective love of God (discerning and do the will of God). 6 & 7 deal with our affective love of God. It is only in the context of our relationship with God (6 & 7) that we can understand the way of surrender.

21. *Oeuvres* V:150-151.

22. *Oeuvres* III:3.

CHAPTER EIGHT

1. For example, not too long after the death of St Francis de Sales, Salesian spirituality unfortunately became tainted by Quietism in a reaction to the rigidity of Jansenism which had become prevalent.

2. Letter of October 13, 1604 in Elizabeth Stopp *Selected Letters*, (London, Faber and Faber 1960) 60.

3. The first edition of *The Introduction to the Devout life* appeared in 1609 and a final edition by Francis in 1619. J. Aumann in *Christian Spirituality in the Catholic Tradition*, San Francisco, Ignatius Press, 1985, 212, writes: 'Perhaps Francis de Sales is the first spiritual writer to comprise a treatise of lay spirituality ... the doctrine taught by him was not new, but he did present spiritual teaching in an original manner and he deserves credit for removing Christian spirituality from the monastic framework in which it had been confined for many centuries.' This acknowledgement that sanctity is for everyone was to be confirmed centuries later in *Lumen Gentium* (n.40) at Vatican II: 'It is evident to everyone that all the faithful of Christ, of whatever rank or status, are called to the fullness of the Christian life and the perfection of charity. By this holiness a more human way of life is promoted, even in this earthly society.'

4. *Oeuvres* III:6.

5. *Oeuvres* XIII:291.

6. *Oeuvres* III:261.

7. *Oeuvres* III:84-85.

8. *Oeuvres* III:20.

9. *Oeuvres* XIV: 53.

10. *Oeuvres* XVIII: 344.

11. *Oeuvres* IV:252.
12. *Oeuvres* III:311.
13. *Oeuvres* XXI:170
14. *Oeuvres* XII:172.
15. *Oeuvres* XIX: 301.
16. Lewis S. Fiorelli, 'Live Jesus: Key aspects of Salesian spirituality' in *Review for Religious*, 46 (Jul/Aug 1987) 499.
17. *Oeuvres* III:133.
18. Letter of October 14, 1604, in Elizabeth Stopp, *Selected Letters*, (London: Faber and Faber, 1960), 72.
19. *Oeuvres* III:260-261.
20. *Oeuvres* XII:206.
21. *Oeuvres* III:22 cf. also III:110;131; 222;305.
22. *Oeuvres* III:24.
23. *Oeuvres* III:262.
24. *Oeuvres* III:135.
25. cf. *Treatise* Book 9.

CHAPTER NINE

1. *Oeuvres* III:322-323.
2. *Oeuvres* III:329-330.
3. *Oeuvres* III:320.
4. Lajeunie Vol. I,186-187.
5. François Favre, Premier Proces Remissorial d'Annecy in Lajeunie vol. I, 487-488
6. *Oeuvres* XIII:233.
7. N. Rogeot, Premier Proces Remissorial D'Annecy in: Lajeunie vol. I, 250.
8. Lajeunie Vol. I, 305.
9. *Oeuvres* Vii:158-159.
10. Lajeunie Vol. 2, 26.
11. Sauzea, Premier Proces Remissorial d'Annecy in: Lajeunie Vol. 2, 234.
12. Michel Favre, Premier Proces Remissorial d'Annecy in Lajeunie Vol. 2, 30-31.
13. There were two centres which promoted devotion to and veneration of St Francis de Sales. These were the regional Seminary of Chieri and the Pastoral Institute in Turin (the Convitto founded in 1817) both of which John Bosco attended. These centres would have helped to promote a popular spirituality to St Francis de Sales in the Piedmont region which John Bosco would have imbibed. His spiritual director, Don Cafasso, in particular, would have encouraged devotion to St Francis de Sales and confirmed him in choosing the saint as patron for his newly-fledged congregation.
14. His *Treatise on The Preventive System* is a form of education based on

reason, religion, and loving-kindness and can be traced to the Pauline exhortation 'Love is patient; Love is kind ... there is no limit to love's forbearance, to its trust, its hope, its power to endure' (1 Cor 13).

15. cf. Arnaldo Pedrini, *S. Francesco di Sales e Don Bosco*, Roma, UPS, 1983, 54.

16. cf. Pietro Braido, in *Ricerche Storiche Salesiane* 8 (1989) n.14, 7-55.

17. *Epistolario di San Giovanni Bosco*, Eugenio Ceria (ed), Vol. 4, 332-333.

18. cf. *Constitutions of the Society of St Francis de Sales*, n. 11, p. 21.

19. When we speak of a school of spirituality we usually mean certain historical periods, currents or groups of people, but according to P. Pourrat, Francis de Sales 'is himself a school of spirituality. He is the beginning, the development and the end.' (*La Spiritualité Chrétienne*. III Les Temps Modernes. Premiäre Partie de la Renaissance au Jansénisme, Libraire V. Lecoffre – J.Gabalda, Paris, 1947, 406).
The most unique expression of the Salesian Spirit is the Visitation Order founded by St Francis de Sales. Nevertheless, the term Salesian Spirituality refers to the many different movements and religious institutes that have imbibed the spirituality of St Francis de Sales. It is this charism of the Salesian Spirit that they have in common, although they give unique expression to it in their various contemplative and active apostolates. Here are some of those associations and institutes that look to Francis de Sales for their inspiration: (1636) Daughters of the Cross; (1740) Sisters of St Francis de Sales (Padua); (1836) Visitation of St Mary of Celles; (1839) Sisters of the Cross of Chavanod; (1859) Salesians of Don Bosco; (1860) Missionaries of St Francis de Sales; (1866) Oblates of St Francis de Sales; (1872) Daughters of Mary Help of Christians (Salesian Sisters); (1876) Salesian Co-operators; (1933) Salesian Sisters of the Sacred Heart; (1964) Secular Institute of St Francis de Sales.

20. St John Bosco adapted the writings of St Francis de Sales when writing for the young, for example, some passages from the *Controverses* are to be found in *Il Cattolico nel Mondo*, 2nd ed, Turin, 1983; extracts from *The Introduction* are present in *Il Giovane Provveduto*, Turin, 1847. Some material from *les Entretiens Sprituels* and also the *Constitutions of the Visitation Sisters* are to be found in *Introduction of the Constitutions and Regulations of the Society of St Francis de Sales*, Turin 1877.

21. *Biographical Memoirs of St John Bosco*, Diego Borgatello (ed. and trans.) vol. XIV:404.

22. cf. A. Pedrini, *St Francis de Sales: Don Bosco's Patron*, New Rochelle, Don Bosco Publications, 1988, 59-68.

23. Jean Pierre Camus, Bishop of Bellery, claimed this was an utterance often on the lips of St Francis de Sales and very much part of his spirit. Don Bosco, in choosing this maxim *'Da mihi animas cetera tolle'* (Give me souls take away the rest), writes that it is 'a motto that

already belonged to St Francis de Sales'. As early as Dec. 1855 Don Bosco had used this motto as an emblem in his circulars. cf. *Biographical Memoirs*, vol. II:410.

24. At the time of his priestly ordination Don Bosco 'takes this motto as his own. He remained faithful to it until death, for he never desired anything but to save as many as possible'. *Biographical Memoirs*, vol. II:410. It is also interesting to note the resolutions that St John Bosco takes before his ordination to priesthood. 'The charity and gentleness of St Francis de Sales are to be my guide:

    1) to accompany and not anticipate the steps of Divine Providence
    2) to ask for nothing; to refuse nothing.' (*Biographical Memoirs*, vol. I:385.)

25. Initially, in secular terms, the Goel meant protecting a relative at a particular time, standing up for and maintaining their rights. E.g. if someone sells a house or piece of property to pay a debt, then the nearest relative is bound to buy back that which was sold and thus restore the possession of the family. Or if someone was murdered, his death shall be avenged (the avenger=Goel) by a relative so that the equilibrium is established again. In religious terms, the Messiah came to be identified as the Goel, to continue the liberation process of Yahweh. Yahweh promised to bring the people out from under the burden of the Egyptians, to deliver them from their bondage and to redeem.

26. Teresa's highest mansion of prayer is identical with Francis's ecstasy of action through charity: 'If the heart stays close with the Lord, it should forget itself entirely; so forgetful of self that one's mind is totally taken up with pleasing him and with discovering new ways to express one's love for him ... this spiritual nuptial is constantly giving birth to good works. We pray not to enjoy it, but with the aim of gathering fresh energy to serve the Lord. Martha and Mary must keep in step, for true hospitality must also give the Lord something to eat. For the soul of prayer is charity, always on the look out for providential opportunities to act or to suffer so that it can please the Lord.'

27. *Oeuvres* IV:301-302.

28. *Oeuvres* III:216-217.

29. Commenting on Francis's use of the word *ouvrage* instead of *oeuvre*, Andre Brix points out that this expresses something very long, and very hard. It is as if Francis de Sales has collected, gathered in a bouquet all the actions of Christ. (*Commentaire*, 415)

30. *Oeuvres* V:14.

31. *Oeuvres* V:11.

CHAPTER TEN

1. *Oeuvres* XX:170.
2. J. W. Crossin, *Friendship the Key to Spritual Growth*, New York, Paulist Press, 1997, 96.
3. *Oeuvres* IV:302.
4. *Oeuvres* IV:256.
5. *Oeuvres* IV:74.
6. The actual term optimism, meaning hopeful, is one which only entered the French language *(optimisme)* in the 18th Century. But of course the tendency and the doctrine expressed by this word are very old, eg. Socrates, Plato, the Stoics – a doctrine expressing that the world is a harmonious whole where everything is admirably ordered.The word *optimisme* was used in French for the first time by the Jesuits of Trevoux, editors of 'memoires pour l'Histoire des sciences et des beaux arts', in the book review of the *Theodicy of Leibniz* – the meaning he gave to optimism is as follows: 'Optimism is a doctrine which claims that this world is the best of all possible worlds: its point of view is that good must always triumph over evil; in other words, optimism is the attitude of mind which always tries to have a large view of everything and which never lets itself despair, even when everything seems to announce defeat.' cf. W. Marceau, 'Optimism in the Works of St Francis de Sales' in *Studies in Salesian Spirituality*, SFS Publications, no. 1, 136-142.
7. *Oeuvres* III:240-241.
8. *Oeuvres* III:68.
9. *Oeuvres* IV:104.
10. *Oeuvres* IV:185.
11. *Oeuvres* III:18.
12. *Oeuvres* IV:184-185.
13. *Oeuvres* IV:186.
14. *Oeuvres* IV:185.
15. *Oeuvres* V:314-315.
16. *Oeuvres* V:315-316.
17. *Oeuvres* V:316.
18. *Oeuvres* XVI:374.
19. *Oeuvres* XIII:207.
20. *Oeuvres* XII:288.
21. *Oeuvres* XIV:57.
22. *Oeuvres* XVIII:172.
23. *Oeuvres* XVI:358.
24. *Oeuvres* V:318.
25. *Oeuvres* VIII:82-83.
26. *Oeuvres* IV:85.
27. Sermon on the Feast of St Mary Magdalen.
28. *Oeuvres* XVIII:172.
29. *Oeuvres* V:314.

CHAPTER ELEVEN

1. cf. Book of Ecclesiasticus.
2. *Oeuvres* III:203-204.
3. cf. *Oeuvres* VI:54-70 Conference on Cordiality. Such an idea in his epoch was seen to be quite radical as it didn't emphasise the juridical aspect of the church but rather the communitarian dimension. For a detailed analysis of this theme, cf. A. Pocetto, 'Ecclesial Dimensions of Salesian Thought'.
4. A. Pocetto, 'Ecclesial Dimensions of Salesian Thought", 2-3.
5. *Oeuvres* IV:208.
6. *Oeuvres* IV:99-100.
7. *Oeuvres* VIII:80. Ash Wed. Sermon, Mar 7th 1612.
8. *Oeuvres* XVIII:415-417, letter to Madame de Villesavin in *Francis de Sales, Jane de Chantal: letters of Spiritual Direction,* W. Wright and J. Power, N.Y., Paulist Press,1988,178.
9. cf. *Oeuvres* I. Les Controverses, A. Pocetto 'The Ecclesial Dimensions of Salesian Thought', 8.
10. *Oeuvres* XV:172.
11. *Oeuvres* III:203.
12. This idea is not original to Francis. Prior to him Richard of St Victor in his *De Trinitate* saw in the Trinity the model of human friendship. Before Francis, St Thomas Aquinas spoke of charity as a love of friendship. In his *Summa Contra Gentiles* he outlines in four chapters (Bk. 4, chs. 15-18) how the Spirit as love effects our lives.
13. *Oeuvres* III:213.
14. *Oeuvres* III:196.
15. *Oeuvres* III:195.
16. *Oeuvres* III:203.
17. *Oeuvres* III:202-203.
18. *Oeuvres* III:203.
19. *Oeuvres* III:202.
20. Fr André Ravier reveals an interesting aspect of Salesian spiritual direction when he entitles his study of St Francis de Sales' letters, *François de Sales. Lettres d'amitié spirituelle* (*Francis de Sales: Letters of Spiritual Friendship*). Such letters are usually referred to as letters of spiritual direction but Ravier justifies the title by explaining that what emerges from these letters is a 'fundamental and essential law of the saint's correspondence', that for Francis spiritual direction cannot be separated from spiritual friendship, 'that is to say there is exchange, communication, reciprocal influence' (Ravier, x).
21. To appreciate the reciprocity of this relationship, read the excellent study by Wendy Wright, *Bond Of Perfection: Jeanne de Chantal and François de Sales,* New York, Paulist Press, 1985.
22. *Oeuvres* XX:216.
23. *Oeuvres* XII:354.
24. Letter to Jane de Chantal, 8 September 1613, in *Oeuvres*: XXI:109.

25. Letter to Jane de Chantal, 22 May 1611, in *Oeuvres*: XV:62.
26. *Oeuvres* XXI:129.
27. H. Bremond, *Sainte Chantal*, Paris, J. Gabalda, 1912, 84. For a more recent biography on the life of Jane de Chantal cf. A. Ravier, *Jane Françoise Fréymot, Baronne de Chantal, Sa Race et Sa Grace*, Paris, Ateliers, Henry Labat, 1983.
28. W. Wright, *Bond of Perfection: Jeanne de Chantal and Francois de Sales*, New York, Paulist Press, 1985, 141.
29. In his Preface to the *Treatise*, he acknowledges the unique contribution of Jane de Chantal, and the Visitation Sisters, saying of her that 'only God knows how I esteem this soul, who has had no little power to animate me in this enterprise', *Oeuvres* IV:21. In his letters to Jane, he consistently informs her of his progress and difficulties in writing the *Treatise* which he calls 'our book', cf. *Oeuvres* XIV:247; 353; XVI:120; 140; 249; 330; XVII:228.
30. *Oeuvres* XVI:128-129.
31. *Sa Vie et Ses Oeuvres*, IV, 115-117: Letter LXV, Annecy, Plon, 1874-1879.
32. P. Serouet, 'François de Sales' in *Dictionnaire de Spiritualité*, Tome V, Paris, Beauchesne, 1964, 1061.
33. F. Vincent, *Saint François de Sales, Directeur d'Ames*, Paris, Beauchesne, 1923, 143.
34. Primitive and definitive editions of the Constitutions in *Oevures*: XXV.
35. W. Wright, *Bond of Perfection: Jeanne de Chantal and François de Sales*, New York, Paulist Press, 1985, 92. Also cf. Francis's own comments on the significance of the Visitation as a name for the congregation, *Oeuvres*: XXV:340.
36. *Oeuvres*: VI:30.
37. *Oeuvres* XX:63.
38. *Oeuvres* III: 207.
39. *Oeuvres* III:50.
40. *Oeuvres* X:240.

CHAPTER TWELVE

1. Chapter VIII of *The Constitution on the Church*, n. 53.
2. *Oeuvres* V:50.
3. Letter to Jane de Chantal, 10 June 1611.
4. A. Pocetto, 'Ecclesial Dimensions of Salesian Thought', 3.
5. First Sermon, written on the Feast of Pentecost, 1593.
6. *Oeuvres* XXVI:266.
7. *Oeuvres* III:104.
8. *Oeuvres* V:287.
9. *Oeuvres* XIV:109.
10. *Oeuvres* III:133.
11. *Oeuvres* III:139.

12. *Oeuvres* III:151.
13. *Oeuvres* III:146-147.
14. *Oeuvres* X:62-63.
15. *Oeuvres* IV:302.
16. *Oeuvres* V:204.
17. The Christian turning to the Father as a child clearly rules out technique in prayer. Technique, as something that one learns and masters, replaces salvation by God. It is contrary to Christian prayer because it is a means of power that wants to meet a goal we have set. The Christian way of prayer is one of obedience, not technique.
18. *Oeuvres* III:106.
19. *Oeuvres* IX:5.
20. Indifference is very much connected with waiting. 'It does not actually will to do a thing, but still it wills to let it be done. The soul that is in this state of indifference wills nothing, but leaves it to God to will what is pleasing to him, must be said to have its will in a simple and general state of waiting ... this waiting on the part of the soul is truly voluntary. Nevertheless it is not an action but rather a simple disposition to receive whatever shall happen. As soon as the events take place and are received, the waiting changes into consent or acquiescence.' *Oeuvres* V:158-159.
21. *Oeuvres* V:183.
22. *Oeuvres* V:121.
23. *Oeuvres* III:171.
24. cf. *Oeuvres* V:55. 'I do not deny that the soul of the most Blessed Virgin had two portions, and therefore two appetites, one according to the spirit and superior reason, and the other according to sense and inferior reason, with the result that she could experience the struggle and contradiction of one appetite against the other. This burden was felt even by her Son.'
25. *Oeuvres* V:52-53.
26. *Oeuvres* V:50.
27. *Oeuvres* V:55.
28. *Oeuvres* III:317.
29. *Oeuvres* III:104-105.
30. *Oeuvres* IV:241.
31. *Oeuvres* V:50-51.
32. *Oeuvres* IX:342.
33. *Oeuvres* III:352.
34. *Oeuvres* III:217.
35. *Oeuvres* III:137.
36. *Oeuvres* III:358.
37. *Oeuvres* III:354.
38. *Oeuvres* XIV:236.